T0114746

# NOT

# MY

# TIME

# TO

# DIE

# NOT MY TIME TO DIE

## A Testimony

YOLANDE MUKAGASANA

WITH PATRICK MAY

Translated from the French by Zoe Norridge

English translation first published in 2019 by
Huza Press
PO Box 1610
Kigali
http://www.huzapress.com
E-mail: info@huzapress.com

First published in France as *La mort ne veut pas de moi* by Éditions Fixot
in 1997

This book is supported by the UK Arts and Humanities Research Council
Global Challenges Research Fund.

ISBN: 978-99977-725-6-5
ebook ISBN: 978-99977-0-098-8

Cover design: Anna Morrison
Cover photography: Chris Schwagga
Typesetting: Margdarshan Productions, India

This book is printed on FSC certified paper.

*In memory of Joseph, Christian,
Sandrine and Nadine.*

Iyo amazi akubwiye ngo winyiyuhagira, urayasubiza
ngo ntambyiro ufite.

If the water says: Don't wash yourself with me! Reply:
I'm not dirty.

Rwandan proverb

# 1

ven if he spends his days elsewhere, Imana returns
every evening to Rwanda. Or so we said. Then the
Catholic missionaries arrived and told us we had to
call him Mungu – God – in Kiswahili. So we called
him Mungu. But soon, at first behind closed doors, then
out loud, we went back to calling him Imana. We began to
worship him again at night. The Rwandan soul rebels against
indoctrination. Make of that what you will.

Does Imana still come to my country every evening to
sleep? And was he with us on the evening of 6 April 1994?
Didn't he abandon us, leave us face to face with the devil?
Perhaps he didn't have time to return to Rwanda on that day.
The night fell so fast.

'How did you manage to hurt yourself so badly?'

'I didn't hurt myself, Muganga! *They* wanted to kill me.
I was walking past the lodgings of the Presidential guard, near
the centre of Kigali. Three soldiers came out and were joined by
a member of the Interahamwe militia armed with a machete.
One soldier asked me for my papers, and the militia man looked
at me suspiciously. "Tutsi! Tutsi!" he shouted. Before I could
move, I felt a sharp pain in my leg and saw the militia man
wiping his machete on the grass. That's all I know, Muganga.'

'What do they want, Makuza*? Surely they're not going
to kill all the Tutsis?'

---

* With the exception of the names of those close to me, all the names of people who
played a role in the events I recount have been changed.

'They'll kill us until the last person is dead. You too, Muganga.'

'You're out of your mind. I'll give you a sleeping pill to help you get some rest tonight. Come back the day after tomorrow for your test results.'

'Yes, Muganga. Goodnight!'

I watch Makuza leave my clinic, dragging his leg, and then carry on working. It's dark outside and the clinic windows mirror my white tunic but not my head, hands and legs, so I look like a puppet dangling from invisible threads. I am a black woman; the windows refuse me my reflection.

I place a few drops of Makuza's blood on a glass slide. Given that he was bleeding anyway, he thought he'd take the chance to find out whether he had malaria. It's routine work and my movements are automatic. I daydream. The blood is taking its own sweet time to dry so I still can't start the analysis.

'These Tutsi men have rebellious blood!' I laugh at my own joke.

I will never see Makuza again.

Sixteen years of marriage. What present should I give to Joseph? In eight days it will be sixteen years of love. Love? Yes, I learned to love over the course of those sixteen years.

Our son, Christian, will soon be fifteen. Christian who dreams of being either the next Platini or a priest, and looks out for his young friends with his amateur karate. Christian, who asks himself questions about death. At his age! Christian, who thinks he knows enough to give me advice. What a kid!

He's the complete opposite of Nadine who's still so scatty, dancing and singing all day long. Nadine, the sunshine of our house, just turned thirteen... already! Once, out of the blue, she asked me a question that I couldn't answer: 'Why is my best friend Hutu?'

And Sandrine, fourteen, my adopted little sweetheart. The good fairy of the house, crazy about cooking and cleaning, meticulous and so shy it's endearing.

As for me, I'm Muganga, doctor. I'm not actually a doctor; I'm a nurse, but I'm in charge. A nurse who manages her own clinic. I have three children, a husband and cousins all over the place: in this country and overseas. I'm Tutsi. That's my biggest mistake. I'm well-off. That's my second. And I'm proud. My third mistake.

My clinic is my pride and joy. It's even been used as a model by the Minister for Health: people come to see it so they can replicate it elsewhere. It exudes cleanliness with its white walls and blue curtains. The only problem is the thin partition that separates my consulting room from the reception area, which means that I have to talk in a low voice. One day I'll build a proper wall.

The telephone interrupts me. Bother! At this time? I've had enough of treating wounded people who tell me the same story: 'I was attacked. They wanted to kill me. They wanted to cut off my arm.'

I don't feel like picking up. I want to think about my children, about the party we're planning together for Joseph, for our wedding anniversary. Should I ask my cousins to come from Butare to dance the night away with us? My thoughts drift away to the sunshine that has flooded the countryside all day long. A happy day, thanks to the sun: Rwanda's most loyal friend. What should I give Joseph? No, I won't pick up the phone; they can call back tomorrow morning.

I pick up.

'Yolande, Yolande! Quick, come home right now. I need to talk to you.'

'What? Joseph! What's going on?'

He's hung up already. I call back but the line is busy. What does he want to tell me?

My husband sometimes plays pranks like this on me when he wants to make love. Several times in the past, when I've been working late at the clinic, he's pretended he needed to see me urgently. When I arrived home, the children were in bed and he'd laid the table just for me. He sat himself down next to me, fed me spoonfuls of stew and laughed: 'You need your strength for the long night we're going to have together.'

We made love all night. In the morning he had the face of a young man again. He called me 'a doctor of the heart as well as the body' and left for work at the Ministry of Transport with a spring in his step.

'Yolande, Yolande! Quick, come home right now. I need to talk to you.'

His words ring in my head. Usually I can guess Joseph's intentions from the sound of his voice. I've been disappointed only once. He had called me home urgently but it wasn't to make love; he wanted to celebrate the surprise arrival of his cousins from Tanzania.

This evening something is different, I sense it in his tone. What's going on? Did Sandrine burn herself while cooking? Does Nadine have a fever? I leave Makuza's blood behind. It will dry on the slide overnight and I'll do the analysis tomorrow.

'Bernard! I'm leaving.'

The night guard appears holding a bowl of rice he's been eating with his fingers.

'Have a nice evening, Muganga!' He looks after everything, in particular, locking up the medicine stores. 'To stop people stealing from you during the night, Muganga.'

'That's right, Bernard. That's right.'

Bernard returns my smile innocently, but I know that he gives out painkillers behind my back. He pretends I've given him permission, as if I trust him enough to dispense medicine in my name. One night the police found him drunk. I had to pay the fine because Bernard, as usual, didn't have any money.

Yes, this is my clinic. I bought all the equipment and medicines myself. I only rent the building. I know people steal from me, I know. But how can you object to that when people can't afford to buy medicine? The only thing that's truly mine is the desire to help people. Indeed, I am a doctor. What I mean is, I'm a nurse who became a doctor because there weren't any doctors nearby. I deal with childbirth, pain relief, even minor operations which are beyond my training, but how can you abandon someone who needs an urgent operation when you know that at the hospital in Kigali he'll wait two or three days on a stretcher before a doctor will so much as listen to his chest? Here in Cyivugiza ward, in the Kigali suburb of Nyamirambo, there is only one clinic – mine. Serving seven hundred people.

It's a little cold. I walk quickly down the path home, five hundred metres at most. Ah look, Nicolas has finally whitewashed the front of his house. About time. I pass two men smoking cigarettes on a bench in front of a wooden house. A little way away some women chat noisily under a shelter made of dried banana leaves. Two teenagers are still out playing, clambering over a henhouse. I greet them: 'Goodnight, my friends!'

Nobody replies. Their eyes avoid mine. They lower their heads as I pass. The two women ignore me and continue their conversation. What's going on? This morning people spoke to me, smiled at me, came to greet me, but this evening they seem to be in on something I'm not.

A light bulb glows weakly in a shed. Four men are playing cards, surrounded by the advice of a fifth and the buzz of mosquitoes. I hear them mutter: 'It's Muganga.'

I feel alone. Am I in danger?

I know what people say about me – that I'm not African enough. Is it because I wear jeans, or because I've only had two children? They say my husband's under my thumb and that one day I'll leave him. Men don't like an emancipated woman, and they like her even less when she has money, white friends, and wears Pierre Cardin glasses. They want to control her; they want to make love to her. How many potential seducers have I had to chase away? Women are wary of me too, but I'm not interested in other people's husbands: mine is enough. The poor love me though, perhaps because they're poor.

I stop for a moment. The opposite hill is lit up by the moon. I think of Masabo, the well-known singer who knows how to evoke the beauty of this 'country of a thousand hills', my country, Rwanda. I walk on, humming. Blessed Rwanda, where Imana comes to rest every evening.

I remember an even older traditional song which recounts how people long ago used to throw young Tutsi girls who fell pregnant into Lake Kivu, with its calm reflective waters surrounded by greenery. One day, Amanda, a beautiful girl from Kibuye, in the west of Rwanda, was condemned to such a death by the family elders. But her grandfather arranged for a dugout canoe to save her in secret and send her to the island of Ijwi. 'In this way,' he said, 'when I look at Ijwi, I'll think of my little Amanda.' It is said that since that day, the Congolese on Ijwi found Tutsi girls so beautiful they went out in canoes to save, ravish and wed them.

It is also said that the Karisimbi volcano never sleeps because it must protect Rwanda. That's just another legend because Karisimbi hasn't erupted for thousands of years. From time to time, its summit is covered with snow. The gorillas that pace its slopes cry like humans, and their little ones, they say, understand the language of flowers.

One of Masabo's songs tells the story of Daliya, a young woman who lives on a hill in the centre of the country. The hill is planted with cassava on successive terraces, like so many of our thousand hills. From the opposite hill, Masabo calls to her, laments her absence, despairs of ever seeing her. His tones are pained and his rhythms seductive, but Daliya remains unmoved. In Rwanda, one hill can provide you with all you need.

And what about the wild animals in the marshes and savannahs of the Akagera Park, do they know they're celebrated by our singers and dancers? The hippopotami, zebras, impalas and topis, the lions, leopards, giraffes and elephants, do they know that Rwandans give up fertile land for them?

Sometimes it seems Masabo's voice depicts my country: it's sharp and nervous at first, like the slopes of the volcanoes, then sweetly undulates, caressing the slopes of the thousand hills, and finally becomes calm and serene as it disappears into the marshes of Tanzania.

# 2

I burst into the dining room.

'Joseph! What are you doing down there? What's going on?'

My husband is crouching on the ground, his back against the wall, his head between his hands. From the ceiling, a bulb shines harshly, moths flutter around it in a disorganized dance. The drinks cabinet is closed, the table isn't laid, the olive-green flowery curtains haven't yet been drawn.

'Joseph, what's wrong with you?'

I bend on one knee before him, like a servant to a king. Slowly he raises his head and looks at me. He is crying.

'Yolande...' The words won't come out. I take his hands. 'Yolande, forgive me!'

'Forgive you? For what?'

'Habyarimana has just been assassinated.'

'Habya...' That's all that comes out of my throat. I drop down in front of him.

We remain like that for a long time, face to face, without saying a word. My uncomfortable position brings me round, I put my hand on the floor to stop myself from toppling over. Outside, a bird sings three reedy notes, descending lower and lower, repeating them obsessively.

'Don't look at me like that, Yolande. I know it's my fault.'

'It's not your fault. You couldn't have known.'

'If I'd agreed to send the children out of the country like you wanted—'

'You couldn't have known.'

I speak in clipped tones, as if I'm afraid of his confession.

In fact, I have already started preparing to flee the country in secret. I've withdrawn all the money in our bank accounts and left some in the clinic's safe, the rest is with the missionaries. Every day I nagged Joseph about leaving. But every day we fell into lengthy discussions which ended with us not making a decision. Just like any normal couple.

Joseph gets up suddenly, paces the room, squashes a mosquito against the wall, exhausting himself with self-recrimination. He shouts, 'I knew it!'

'Calm down! Inzira ntibwira umugenzi. If the road gave directions to the traveller, nobody would get lost.'

'But I knew it! I've killed my children! The children are as good as dead. Blame me!' With each phrase he hits the table in frustration.

'For the last three years everyone has known Habyarimana's plans. For the last eight months the radio has been inciting Hutus to kill Tutsis. And for the last three months, we've known that Habyarimana has been overpowered by the extremist wing of his own party. We knew that they were preparing for a massacre. I knew it, but I just didn't want to see it!'

Joseph falls into a wicker chair and cries like a child, beaten, powerless, overcome with sadness and rage.

'I knew it, Yolande, I knew it. But I didn't want to believe it. Who could imagine that in such a small country, where we speak the same language and share the same traditions...'

He implores me with his eyes. He would like me to tell him that all is not lost.

'All is not lost,' I say out of cowardice, but I don't believe it. If only he would stop crying!

Nepo, my brother, rushes in. He stops and stares at me with wide eyes. His face is even thinner than usual. We cry together. He takes my hands and squeezes them.

There's a gunshot in the distance. Joseph runs into the garden, but there's nothing to see except the darkness of the Rwandan night, the countryside dotted with lights, the road lit up by the neighbours' homes, and the glinting stars.

'Yolande,' Nepo says, 'I have a feeling everything is over.'

He takes my palm slowly but firmly, as if he wants to open a reluctant shell: 'Look at this hand... Look, and listen to what I see.'

He turns, glances out at the garden, where Joseph has clambered onto a table to see further. I wait, my hand open. Just then, Sandrine appears, terrified, her adolescent body outlined in the doorway, slender and nimble. She is only thirteen, but already she turns men's heads in the street.

'Bring us some flour, little one!' Nepo commands in his diviner's voice.

I laugh at his calling my daughter 'little one'. It's what we used to call Sandrine, but it makes no sense now. Sandrine is even taller than me. But then as I look at her I want to cry. If I hadn't adopted her when her mother died, perhaps she wouldn't be in danger today.

'Flour? But why?' she asks.

'Flour, I tell you!'

Sandrine moves off gracefully and reappears with a small bag of cassava flour. Nepo plunges his hand into the bag, takes out a pinch of flour, and places it on my palm.

'Go, Sandrine, for just a moment. I don't want to prophesy in front of children.'

Sandrine backs away, terror in her eyes.

'Go, little one,' I say softly. 'Leave us.'

'Mama, how can you send me away when I love you?'

'You won't understand. I'll call you back in a bit.'

She leaves, and we hear her footsteps in the kitchen; no doubt she's spying on us. Finally, she closes the door.

'Do you see this flour, Yolande?'

There's a small mound of white flour in the palm of my hand.

'It looks likes the summit of Kilimanjaro,' I smile.

'This flour is your loved ones: Joseph, Christian, Sandrine, Nadine. It's me too, our sisters and all your cousins.'

Nepo blows violently on my palm. The flour disappears. All that's left is a fine off-white film, more visible in the creases of my hand.

'Where is the flour now?'

'Blown away! What a question!'

'Blown away. That's how your loved ones will disappear. You will lose us all and you will remain alone. Because it's not your time to die. You will soon lose everything except love. You will lose your faith, hope and confidence, but you will never lose love. And you will avenge us.'

I don't want to believe it.

'How can you be so sure Habyarimana's death will start a Tutsi massacre?' I rage. I get up and clap my hands violently to shake off what's left of the flour. I laugh in despair. 'There will be no massacre!'

But I don't believe what I say. I know that the apocalypse Colonel Bagosora announced when he returned from Arusha, after the signing of the peace agreement, has begun. I know, just like Joseph. And, like Joseph, I don't want to believe it.

My husband returns: 'I can't see anything. Perhaps there's nothing to fear tonight. Calm down, Yolande.' He begins to tremble like a leaf. He's the one who needs calming down.

The phone rings. Friends from Masaka, not far from Kigali, confirm that the Interahamwe are already going from house to house, killing Tutsis. I hang up, incredulous. I turn on the radio. One of Bikindi's endless songs.

'Children of crop-growers, be vigilant,' he yells in rhyming verse, like rap, intercut with choruses sung by girls who vow that they are indeed vigilant.

The news, at last. But no, this isn't the news. 'Make use of your machetes!' shouts the presenter. 'Put up roadblocks. No snake should escape your grasp. You are working for the future and glory of your country. Learn how to recognize and cut down our internal enemy; he who has stolen from us and enslaved us for centuries.'

A call to kill. Joseph and I look at each other, petrified.

Nepo suggests we flee with his family. We agree. He'll come back for us in fifteen minutes. We gather together a few things and close the windows in a hurry; we are already exiles. We hear my brother's minibus and go outside in silence, carrying our clothes and some cold chicken. The children are bewildered by this impromptu trip. They ask for explanations. We don't reply.

'Get into the minibus as fast as possible, without drawing attention to yourselves and lie down under the seats.'

There are at least twenty of us in the vehicle, all Tutsis, sitting one on top of the other. Parents, children, cousins and my sister Hilde, who has been staying with us for the past week. We know this is a dangerous undertaking. We have to drive around Mount Kigali, skirt the centre of town, and then cross the bridge over the Nyabarongo River to get to the road to Butare. It will take us fifteen minutes if we're lucky to leave Kigali.

The minibus hurtles off, wheezing as it bounces through potholes. We pass by the houses of our neighbours. Their dining rooms are lit and I can make out people's shadows. Two women are chatting, each in her own kitchen, raising their voices across the bamboo fence. Further down is Déo's house, set back a little and diagonal to the road. Then a large expanse of darkness: the plantation near Côme's place. We pass by my clinic, its security light is on. Bernard must be at the bar next door. There is the imposing residence of the Deputy Prefect, its front illuminated. We round the corner and leave Cyivugiza, my ward. Opposite us, Mount Kigali is dotted with lights like stars in the sky. After driving for five minutes on dirt roads, we reach the tarmac that leads to the South and on to Burundi. to us, it has been more like three hours.

'Kankindi we!'

'What's going on, Nepo?'

My brother doesn't reply, he makes an acrobatic half-turn that shakes us around like beans in a sieve. He only calls on my mother's name like this when he's alarmed.

'I saw soldiers over there, we would have got ourselves killed. We're going back home.' Our faces freeze with fear and our hearts are heavy as we head back. My brother drops us off. 'There's nothing more we can do, Yolande, except wait.'

'Wait for what?'

'For death.'

'Nepo, let's not lose courage, we'll get out of this.'

'You, yes, you will get out of this, Yolande, because it's not your time to die. But I know the rest of us will die. The flour said so.'

'The flour said nothing!'

'I know, Yolande. I know.'

I watch him get back into his minibus. His family hides just below the windows. You'd think he was a lone man, driving an empty bus. Will I see Nepo again?

I pull myself together and call the UN military headquarters, the famous MINUAR – United Nations Assistance Mission for Rwanda. 'We can't help you, Madam. Forgive us.'

The United States Embassy has a similar response, as does the Belgian Embassy. They say that they can't intervene until people have been hurt. The International Red Cross can do nothing either. I call the Vatican representatives, they hang up. I call Parliament, where the rebels are located. They were installed there officially, after the signing of the Arusha Peace Agreement, which imposed multi-party democracy. The phone line has been cut.

There is no more hope. We must wait our turn. We must prepare ourselves and the children to accept everything: torture and then death.

I gather the children together and talk to them in a clumsy ceremonial tone. 'My children, I know that you won't be able to understand what I'm going to say to you now, but I'm asking you to obey me. Tonight we're going to sleep in the bush.'

They protest. Sandrine doesn't want to sleep outside. Nadine is afraid of caterpillars and snakes. Thankfully, Christian interrupts them briskly with his child's voice that's only just beginning to break: 'Only God will decide what happens to us. Mama is right. We will sleep in the bush tonight, and God will protect us.'

His words are like an order. The girls obey with tears in their eyes, each one taking the blanket he throws over their shoulders.

'Nadine,' Christian calls to his sister, 'bring the chocolate we were saving for my birthday.'

We leave by the garden. Joseph forces a way through the fence of bulrushes held together with barbed wire and we slip into the bush one after the other, my sister Hilde bringing up the rear.

'Yolande,' she says, 'I didn't dare tell you. The Interahamwe have already put up barricades everywhere. They're calling them roadblocks, but they're not much more than stones laid across the road to hold up cars. They've been there talking all day long, and I heard them say that they wanted to go to the clinic and cut you down. They're afraid you will treat the rebel soldiers when they arrive. They even thought about calling you and pretending there was an emergency to lure you into a trap. You must hide.'

'They've tried that already. They called me two months ago, saying that there was a woman in labour. Of course this woman didn't exist and luckily I became suspicious just in time. I've been wary ever since it was claimed on the radio that I went to Uganda to do a course on how to kill Hutus by injection, when really I had gone to buy medicine that wasn't available here in Kigali. But Hilde, why did you wait so long to tell us there were roadblocks?'

'I didn't dare. I didn't want to discourage you.'

'Discourage me? Do you think I can be discouraged?'

We move forward carefully, bent over so that the grass can hide us. Crickets fall silent as we pass. Hilde sneezes, we freeze. A stone's throw away, a window opens and a silhouette stands out against the light; it seems to be peering into the bush. The window closes again. We move on until we reach a dense thicket where Christian liked to hide out and play when he was younger, watching and waiting for me to come home.

It's pitch black. We set up camp without seeing a thing, falling into silence as if all words are useless. Once we are still, the crickets begin to sing again.

Legend has it that a long time ago, Gihanga came down from the sky to the heart of Rwanda and had three sons: Gahutu, Gatutsi and Gatwa. Gahutu liked the earth and its fruits, Gatutsi reared cattle and Gatwa spent his days working with clay. The three brothers loved each other. Gahutu shared cereals to eat, Gatutsi offered milk from his herd and Gatwa transported food from one brother to the other in his plates and jugs. At that time the Hutu, Tutsi and Twa were still brothers. What went wrong?

Another of our legends is about Urutare rwa Kamegeri, Kamegeri's Rock.

It seems to me that the violent history of modern Rwanda began the day the King asked his courtiers for advice about how to put a traitor to death. Kamegeri stood up: 'Lord, heat the rock by the roadside, and let us leave the guilty person there; he will be burnt alive.'

The King replied: 'Kamegeri, since you are capable of imagining such cruelty, let this torture be yours!'

The zealous accuser was taken to the rock and he perished there, burned to death. Ever since then, the rock has carried his name.

My country's legends may seem cruel to some but they simply express the popular imagination. We Rwandans are not afraid of cruelty: it's part of our lives. So much so that it makes us laugh that France has abolished the death penalty.

'Ishuli' is one of the only words left behind by German colonization, but it's an important one, it means 'school'. As for the Belgians, they taught us to hate each other, with the support of the Church. 'Tutsis are the superior race,' said the colonizers. 'Hutus, who make up ninety per cent of the population, are Bantu peasants, slow and simple, without a thought for the future.'

Eh! But I am Tutsi! Perhaps that's why today I must pay for the sins of my ancestors, who ruled over the country for four centuries, until 1959, when we had our 'French Revolution': one social class pitted against another. They tried to pass it off as an inter-ethnic struggle, but it wasn't. Even today, the Rwandan struggle isn't inter-ethnic, it's intra-ethnic: brothers killing brothers. If Gihanga only knew...

# 3

gunshot wakes me. It was faint, at a distance, but still, it woke me. That said, I'm not sure I was sleeping. I don't know any more. Drowsing, perhaps.

A light wind caresses my face with honeysuckle breaths. My three children are sleeping with clenched fists. At least that's what I think until I notice Nadine's eyes shining. She's at my feet, her arm around my ankles, like a defeated fighter begging for mercy. Sandrine and Christian are further away, tensed up on top of their blankets, breathing irregularly, almost panting. No, they're not sleeping, they're frozen with fear.

There are no caterpillars or snakes here. All seems calm, save for that gunshot in the distance, a few whistles, the sound of a car driving somewhere, and now and then, the dull thud of a grenade exploding far away on the opposite hill.

In Rwanda, the stars shine more brightly than elsewhere. It's because of the altitude, I think. I look at the stars to stop my mind filling with worry. There's the Southern Cross. I love my children, but do I love them enough to save them?

Joseph is resting, leaning the nape of his neck on a tree stump. He's not really sleeping, but he's breathing heavily. Hilde sits against a tree, her legs stretched out in front of her, her eyes gazing upwards to the stars, like a drunken sailor propped up against a mast. A strong sweet smell of bananas grips me, overpowering the scent of hibiscus flowers around us. There must be a marsh behind us: I can hear frogs croaking softly.

We Rwandans live close to nature. Only the whites would pity us that! We can live for days off passion fruit and wild raspberries; we can catch a hare with our bare hands; we make traps for partridges and even antelopes, from creepers or banana fibre. We treat our illnesses with herbs or roots. We don't just like nature, we are nature. Nature calls and smiles at us. But tonight she is not smiling, or perhaps I'm no longer able to see her smiling.

Out of habit, my fingers stroke the small scar that I've had forever on my right thigh. It's a raised straight line that marks a dip in the skin, a sign that I've grown. The whole length is dotted with little cracks, like the lips of an old woman.

When I touch this scar, I see bare-chested men with dried banana leaves on their backs and armbands in red or green, brandishing spears and machetes. 'Where is your husband?' they ask my mother. She doesn't reply. They search the house. They break a clay pot of milk, and I begin to cry. I'm five years old; I sob into my mother's skirts. 'Where is your husband?' they ask again. One of them yanks me away from my mother, throws me to the ground, holds me down with a foot on my chest: bare and dirty, hardened from direct contact with the earth, and riven with cracks as sharp as nails. They shout at Mama: 'So you won't talk? You don't want to talk? Look!' One of the men plunges the tip of his spear into my thigh. Blood spurts out. 'Tell us!' My mother remains silent. The man pulls out the spear and they all flee, terrified by my mother's defiance. That was in 1959, in Save, the village where I was born, during the Hutu revolution that brought Grégoire Kayibanda to power.

When the murderers couldn't find my father and brothers, they turned on the cattle, hitting them to chase them off so they could kill and eat them. One of our cows had recently given birth and had so much milk. She refused to leave and went instead to her calf who was crying out in distress. My mother and I were alone in the house, terrified and unable to move.

One of the men shouted at the cow: 'So you won't come out? Well then, we'll kill you and your calf right here, and take the meat.' He dealt a machete blow to its neck and it staggered. A second horizontal blow cut across her haunches. Blood spurted out, the cow fell, and trickles of milk mixed with the blood at her feet. From that day on I couldn't drink milk: it felt like I was drinking blood.

When they left, I asked Mama: 'Is there no good milk left at all? Not in Rwanda, not in the rest of the world?'

'No, Yolande, there is only sour milk left.'

Mama took me to the forest and found herbs to treat my wound. I was in so much pain I cried in silence. My leg healed, thanks to my mother's traditional medicine. Afterwards, I told her: 'I'm going to be a nurse. I want to look after people.'

Rwanda has been in a permanent state of genocide, of never-ending massacres. I was five in 1959, nine in 1963 when there were massacres in Bufundu Gikongoro, thirteen in 1967 for the massacres in the Bugesera. In 1973 when there were killings across the country, I was nineteen. There were massacres in Kibirira in 1990, in the Bugesera in 1992, of the Abagogwe Tutsis in Ruhengeri in 1993, and so many others. So many genocides unpunished and ignored by the UN and the world.

Must my children live in a country that is visited by genocide in everlasting cycles, like an exterminating angel that never gives up? They didn't even know they were Tutsi before they were twelve! They learned about it the day the Minister of Education decided to separate Tutsi and Hutu children in schools. Poor Nadine didn't understand why her best friend at school was Hutu; she couldn't see any differences between Hutus and Tutsis. And yet she was regularly humiliated in class for being Tutsi, just like I was throughout my schooldays. Pro-Hutu headmistresses even lowered my marks without the teachers knowing. Much later, Hutu ministers offered me nursing jobs forbidden to Tutsis in exchange for special services. I always refused.

Distraught, my mind roams through my childhood memories at random and I see scenes of torture, assassination, corruption, blackmail. People become racist when they can no longer explain their own unhappiness. This quasi-philosophical idea comforts me for a moment; I enjoy it in secret before it disappears. No, I will never be able to explain what is happening to us this evening, in the bush, hiding from our neighbours; the same neighbours who smiled at us just a few days earlier.

The lights go on in our house. A man wearing a beret looks around. He has a machete shoved under his belt. Our two guard dogs bark like mad and tug at their chains. After only a minute, the man leaves the house and walks around the garden. He kneels at the place where we broke the hedge, then goes back towards the house and disappears from view down the road.

I begin to daydream again. I see the party we had at our neighbours' house four years ago. The war of 1990 had just ended with what the government called the bitter failure of the Rwandan Patriotic Front, the famous RPF, although in reality it was just a change in tactic, with the Front opting for guerrilla warfare rather than direct confrontation. A guerrilla war that has gone on for four years now.

That day, my husband had become godfather to his cousin's newborn, so we were all in our Sunday best. The head of the family had just finished his speech, and we were chatting, telling jokes and laughing, when an army car pulled up, raising a large cloud of dust. Three soldiers pulled our cook, Yozefu, out of the car in handcuffs. Yozefu, afraid and crying, pointed out my husband with a nod of his head. Immediately, the soldiers removed the handcuffs from him and put them on my husband. They took Joseph to the 'forensics' department: the torture chamber of the state police in Kigali. Our party was disrupted, the guests were in tears, absolutely terrified. Two hours later the soldiers came back and took me and the three children to the 'forensics' buildings. There, we learnt it was all because of a trifle: a pair of binoculars that my children used to look at animals. The soldiers claimed we had bought them to give to the rebel forces when they arrived in Kigali.

Somehow, by some miracle, they finally let us go. Thinking about it now, my head throbs with the hope of seeing the rebel forces arriving, the squabbles of daily life, and the arbitrary humiliation all mixed together. For four years we've been living with uncertainty, unable to feel safe but not quite ready to leave. I start crying. Hot silent tears fall slowly down my cheeks as if my body is cleansing itself. I want to die. But no, I want to live.

The crickets fall silent. Someone's there. I hold my breath and listen. Joseph is snoring lightly now. I don't dare move, I don't dare call out. I lean backwards carefully and grope around the ground until I find a dead branch. I lift it up silently and manage to prod Joseph's arm. He sits up. I position my face in profile so that he can see my movements outlined against the sky, and place a finger on my mouth. Joseph understands. He places a hand on the children to warn them to breathe as quietly as possible. We stay like this for three or four minutes, completely still. Hilde coughs. I lean towards her and pinch her, almost out of spite. She gets the message. We hear a noise, like a blade cutting grass. I tremble. Nadine reacts, hides her head in my lap. I whisper to be quiet. Another swish.

Suddenly I see a large man wearing a small beret walking slowly, calmly, silhouetted against the Milky Way. The machete he is holding in one hand shines in the moonlight. Now and then, he sweeps it up towards the sky and down again into the grass. He passes by without seeing us. An owl hoots behind me; the man turns towards us. I instinctively close my eyes so that they don't shine in the dark. Carefully, I place my hands over my face and open my fingers. I reopen my eyes and watch the man approach. I'm terrified. He is now only six or seven metres away. He stops and peers in our direction for a long time. It is the longest minute of my life. Then he turns around and continues walking as before, swiping his machete up and down.

The crickets begin their concert again, and I thank Imana for having created these little creatures that warn us when an enemy is near. 'Mana! Mana! Will you please protect my children?' I plead silently.

My mind roves back to the hundreds of events in my life as a Rwandan Tutsi. Right now, I can't pin down the order in which they happened, recall my state of mind, or even the exact nature of the events themselves. I'm tortured by this relentless pain, the certainty that this is the end, the certainty that this isn't the end. Is Rwanda still my country? I imagine us finding refuge in Uganda; Joseph, my children and I. Or in Belgium, if need be. I see myself working in a hospital in Brussels, dealing with another kind of racism. The proverb says, umutima wuzuye amaganya ntusobanura amagambo — a heart drowning in sadness can't describe its pain. O, my Rwanda, don't abandon me!

Our house lights turn on again. This time it's four or five soldiers inspecting my sitting room. Our dogs bark but are silenced by two gunshots. More windows light up. I hear cries, laughter, as if the soldiers are telling each other salacious jokes. They're enjoying themselves. I see them move around the sitting room, their enormous shadows etched onto the walls like monsters. I'm less afraid now; drunken soldiers don't know how to kill, at least I hope they don't. After about fifteen minutes they go, leaving the sitting-room light on.

The night is coming to an end as the Southern Cross pales, surrounded by light, like a halo. I look for the moon's profile, but it has turned its face away. I can already see the faint shape of the Muhabura volcano on the horizon, the frontier between Rwanda and Uganda. How many kilometres separate us? Sixty? Seventy? To be so close to freedom and yet unable to reach it!

The Milky Way has completely disappeared. Hutus only kill at night, I reassure myself, because they're afraid of killing. Right now an absolute calm reigns. Even killers need to sleep.

# 4

**W**hen we return home we're greeted by a few empty beer bottles and a bottle of whisky, nicely arranged on the living-room table. Six in the morning and it's just getting light.

The children watch the deserted road while I rush to the radio. Radio Rwanda is playing classical music, meaning the nation is in mourning. I change the station to RTLM: Radio Télévision Libre des Mille Collines. Despite its name, the television station has never existed: it's just radio. 'Libre' means 'free' but really it's in the pockets of those in power. 'Mille collines' — yes, my country has a thousand hills, and we live on one of them, but for how much longer? My loved ones and I have a suspended death sentence. In fact, I am already dead: dead to the freedom of life.

RTLM broadcasts an Adventist song. The last chords fade away and a neutral voice follows, listing the deaths of the night: 'The prefecture of rural Kigali, commune of Kanzenze, sector of Ntarama, dead: ...' Four names are announced with joyful hatred. 'Prefecture of Byumba, commune of Kibari, sector of Buhambe, dead: ...' Three names. 'Prefecture of Gitarama, commune of Mushubati, sector of Remera, dead: ...' Seventeen names, an entire family.

It sounds like a late-night broadcast of election results just in from the counting. They don't mention the prefecture of Butare, where I was born and where nearly all my family lives. Could it be that there were no killings there?

A musical interlude. We're treated to Bikindi and his murderous songs once more. Then, with a monstrous, authoritative voice, Kantano, the best presenter at the station, calls listeners to go murder. One of his associates presses the point: 'Let us revenge the appalling assassination of the much-loved Juvénal Habyarimana by these cockroaches, and let us revenge, at the same time, that of Melchior Ndadaye, the late President of Burundi, on 21 October 1993. Track the snakes everywhere and kill them. May your magnificent work free the world from evil!'

A third partner-in-genocide adds with a serious voice and dry tone: 'How can you tell the cockroach from a Hutu? In lots of ways:

The cockroach has gaps between his front teeth.

The cockroach has narrow heels.

The cockroach has eight pairs of ribs.

The female cockroach has stretch marks on her thighs, near her buttocks.

The cockroach has a narrow nose.

The cockroach has less kinky hair.

The cockroach's skull is long at the back and his forehead is sloped.

The cockroach is tall and has a haughty look.

The male cockroach has a pronounced Adam's apple.'

Music once again, this time, a group from Zaïre. The rhythm is catchy, frenzied, almost mindless.

'Remember', booms another voice, 'that the Arusha Peace Agreement, that worthless piece of paper, has been definitively consigned to the country's past. Remember that the multi-party state was imposed by the whites. Remember the hateful presence of MINUAR, the force that tried to prevent us from managing our own affairs. Remember the near victory of the rebels a year ago; they almost took Kigali. Therefore, every Hutu family, every single Hutu, has a duty to his country today. And this duty is simple: to exterminate the cockroaches. May your machetes serve you well! And may every Hutu who gets the chance to kill a serpent but does not, be killed in his turn. You must forget your political allegiances; you, children of crop farmers, are all the same, and you have a sole common enemy: the cockroach.'

Music again. Masabo, my favourite musician, sings about the country of a thousand hills, the volcanoes of the North, the hills in the Centre, the plains of the East. He paints the contours of Rwanda with his tune. But Masabo, why are you on RTLM? Are you a traitor as well? You, whose sensual songs I hummed only yesterday, would you kill Tutsis too?

A voice that I think I recognize but can't place announces a new list of names. In Gisenyi, two priests were killed by nurses. In Kigali, people have been found dead in a hospital. Each time, the Patriotic Front is held responsible for the massacres. The presenter claims they left the Parliament buildings without permission.

In the prefecture of the town of Kigali, commune of Nyarugenge, sector of Nyamirambo, dead: Kayijuka Théoneste, Rukera Stanislas, Mulindwa Épaphrodite, Mukarwego Antoinette and her daughter Mukandoli Françoise, Muganga Mukagasana Yolande, dead from complications due to injuries, at Kigali Hospital.

Yes, that's it, I do know this presenter. But what is his name?

Joseph turns to me. 'What's going on? They've announced your death!'

I lower my head, almost ashamed not to be dead.

The phone rings, making us jump. A friend offers his condolences to Joseph; he's just heard about my death. My husband thanks him and asks him to wait a moment. I take the receiver. 'It's me, Yolande. I, who am supposed to be dead!'

I break into nervous laughter. I want to shout: 'It's me, Muganga Yolande Mukagasana, I'm alive.'

Instead, I cry.

'Who said I was dead?'

'Noël Hitimana.'

'Noël? Was that him on the radio?'

'You know him?'

'Do I know him? He's a neighbour.'

All my hot-blooded black womanhood suppressed by the missionaries comes back to the surface. 'This journalist who said I was doing courses in Uganda on how to kill the Hutu? This journalist whose balls I'm going to cut off? Do I know him? I'd like to live for a hundred years in a room with his balls on display, cooking slowly above the fire. I'd smoke them for a long time, and afterwards, eat them.'

I break down. 'No, no, I'm sorry, I don't want to eat Noël's balls, I'm upset, nothing more.' I let the receiver go.

Who was that on the phone?

The radio exudes hatred. What hurts me most is that they never say the word 'Tutsi'. They talk about serpents, cockroaches, enemies, traitors, but they don't name us. I'd like an enemy who has the courage to say who I am: Tutsi. Muganga Tutsi. Muganga Yolande Mukagasana, Tutsi. It's because they don't announce my ethnicity that I feel so sad and alone. I am proud, proud to be Tutsi.

The presenter orders people to erect roadblocks: 'Every man across the entire country should guard his roadblock. Every Tutsi, every Hutu, shall present himself at the nearest roadblock. The man who doesn't go to his roadblock will be considered a traitor. Each roadblock has its leader who will update everyone on their duties. It is forbidden for anyone to leave their district. Ask people you don't know for their identity card. If they're cockroaches, catch them. The roadblock leader will tell you what to do with them.'

I fall into Joseph's arms and we cry for a while.

'But they're mad!'

'I don't know, Joseph. I don't understand anything.'

'They can't really be asking Tutsis to present themselves at the roadblocks so that they can be massacred!'

Joseph sobs, 'I want to live, Yolande. I don't want to go and get myself killed...'

His words hang suspended in silence.

'We need to do something, Joseph!'

'What?'

'I don't know.'

'Me neither.'

I shout: 'Do something! Make a decision! Act, damn it!'

'But I don't know what to do.'

'Yes you do, you want to die.' I'm furious. I stamp my feet; I want to slap my husband.

'Yolande, I beg you, calm down.'

'I'm going mad, Joseph.' It's my turn to burst into tears. 'Joseph, I'm sorry! I no longer know what I'm saying. But do something, I beg you. These people are sadists! They'll make us obey their short-sighted plan like sheep. They're sick. Do something.'

Joseph places his hand on my cheek. I hate his tenderness; the tenderness of a man who no longer knows how to act. 'Listen, Yolande, this is what we're going to do.'

'What?'

'You and the children will hide in the bush. I'll go to the roadblock since I don't have a choice. But I will try to get away from time to time to bring you provisions.'

My husband has taken a decision, perhaps the biggest decision of his life. I'm seized with pride. I'm loved. A man is worrying about me and the children he gave me. I feel like a woman again.

'You know, Yolande, as long as they haven't found you, they'll leave me alive so that I can betray you.'

'But why do they want *me*?'

'Because you're the most high-profile woman in the district.'

'Me?'

'Yes, you! You know it well! I love you, Yolande.'

We live like this for five days, between the bush and the house, without being able to go further, hardly able to feed ourselves. The irony is that it's less dangerous to go to the house during the day than at night because they think we won't dare enter in the daytime, so they don't bother looking for us then. At night, the house is visited regularly. Soldiers took our car on the first night. And Hilde, my sister Hilde, decides one morning to leave us.

'It doesn't matter, in the end, if they kill me!' she says. 'It's no longer important! I'm leaving to hide by myself because I don't want to put the children in danger. It's better that we spread ourselves out in the bush.'

I hug her. I have a feeling I'll see her again. I'm not afraid for her. I even smile.

'Where do you find the strength to smile?' she asks me, almost jealous.

I don't reply.

A roadblock made up of a few branches thrown across the road is erected close to our house, in front of the neighbouring bar. Men guard it in shifts, day and night. It's the second roadblock in the district. Another, they say, has been put up near my clinic. One night, I approach the roadblock to listen to the soldiers' talk. A rifle shines in the light from the bar, drunken men roar with laughter and smoke cannabis rolled into shapeless cigarettes. I hear them swear that they'll get Muganga. They tell one another all sorts of fantastic stories about me: that I'm a rebel, an informant for the rebels in Uganda. I'm even a captain in the RPF.

A soldier arrives for his shift holding a bottle of beer in his hand. He spits on the ground and wipes his mouth with the back of his sleeve. 'What are you talking about?'

'Muganga.'

'Eh! I've heard all sorts of things about her.'

'Like what?'

'Listen, little one, you're still young. But listen well! You know Dallaire?'

'The leader of the Blue Berets?'

'Yes! Well, I've heard that Muganga is his mistress!'

Dallaire! What a joke! I don't even know what he looks like.

The young one assumes an understanding air. 'I know something too. They say she has long breasts shaped like bananas, like all Tutsi women.'

The men laugh. But then a woman cries out: 'I'd like to have the honour of cutting off her breasts while she's still alive! Promise me that if you find Muganga, you'll call me before killing her.'

A man swears to honour the request. The woman thanks him.

Eh! I know this woman: Espérance Mayimuna, a girl who works at Air Rwanda. Cut off my breasts? What a strange desire!

Like all men, my husband must guard the roadblock nearest to his home, but he only spends a few hours there each day. He comes and goes between the roadblock and the bush like a badly behaved schoolchild. He is resigned to it; he doesn't know the day he'll die, all he knows is that it's coming.

'Why don't they kill you straight away?' I wonder.

'Because they know that the whole district is sealed off, so we won't be able to escape anyway.'

'In other words, they might as well let us live in fear for a few more days before the apocalypse.'

We now live in a space made up of our house, a bit of bush and some plantations, but we're fenced in on all sides. The Hutus can laugh at us living in horror for a few more days. Perhaps they even hope that Joseph will start killing his fellow Tutsis in the end.

Each time he goes back to the roadblock they ask him where I am. He invariably replies that I fled with the children; that's all he knows. Sometimes a soldier slaps or punches him. 'You're making fun of me, Joseph. You know very well where she is.'

He tells me, 'As long as they haven't found you, they'll keep me alive to try and get me to speak. As long as you're not found, I'm safe.'

The massacres have spread throughout the country except in the prefecture of Butare, the university town in the South. Every morning, the radio presenter reads endless lists with an icy voice. Sometimes I hear the names of friends or cousins. One morning, the radio contradicts the news of my death. This is bad luck: now the fanatics will start looking for me again.

I want to find out more, so I continue to spy on the roadblock, hidden within a rifle's reach, almost nose to nose with my enemies. They say I disguised myself as a nun and rejoined the RPF rebels in Rebero, the hill opposite this one. Apparently, I give myself to the rebel soldiers to encourage them to fight.

A soldier turns on the radio, lets it blast out across the district. I learn that Rwanda has a new President, Théodore Sindikubwabo, whose passion is making forceful speeches calling for genocide: 'Let us congratulate our courageous army who have brought security back to the country... The soldiers and the government have agreed on how to rule the country... You are the most numerous and therefore, according to the law, I will support you...'

The presenter resumes: 'Dear citizens, remember, the Hutu Ten Commandments: a Hutu must never feel pity for a Tutsi; the Tutsi is dishonest in business; every Hutu must spread the current ideology...' and on he reads.

A song by that bastard, Bikindi, comes on. Never again will I listen to Bikindi.

I crawl back from my expedition, passing by the house to get one or two avocados, some sugar and a little rice that I cook in a hurry. My children are wilting, Christian and Sandrine have long faces. Nadine is more resilient, but as for me, I'm unrecognizable. The skin on my stomach and thighs is withering, and I talk about my glasses, my wedding ring and my little radio all the time. I lost all three the first night we spent in the bush and I look for them obsessively.

My only hope is that the rebels reach our hill soon. It seems they've already taken the one opposite. Why are they taking so long to come?

What is RTLM saying now? I return to the roadblock. Between songs the presenter cautions: 'Bene Sebahinzi murabe maso, sons of Sebahinzi, be careful.' For us Rwandans, 'Sebahinzi', used as a proper noun, means 'the father of the crop farmer'. All Rwandans know that crop farmers are Hutu, just like we know that 'cockroach' or 'snake' refers to the Tutsi. In this way, a phrase that foreigners think is harmless takes on a very particular meaning. For those who don't speak our language, the genocide is indecipherable. Intolerance has always been built upon metaphor, and Kinyarwanda is a language where this reigns supreme. Is that why Western powers didn't block the calls to genocide on RTLM? Some Belgian journalists even supported this sham of a free radio. Out of ignorance, perhaps?

# 5

amafis is a Tutsi woman who gave birth in my clinic at the end of March. She's a widow who remarried a Hutu widower and they love each other to distraction. They have three children from their first marriages and two from their second. Their last born is called Mpore, named after my clinic, which means, more or less, consolation. The husband, Anastase, is a moderate Hutu, but his brother is in the Presidential Guard and is a member of an extremist party. No wonder the two hate each other. A month or two ago, I heard them quarrelling.

'There's no sense in calling yourself Hutu. Grandfather was Tutsi. He became Hutu only because he lost his cattle through negligence. Hutu and Tutsi are not races, nor are they ethnicities. They're castes, so to speak: social categories.'

'Oh, for goodness sake, Anastase. What does your identity card say? That you're Hutu, no?'

'Identity cards are a Belgian invention — they didn't understand anything about our constantly changing society.'

'A Belgian invention? Eh! Your wife is clearly Tutsi! Just look at her: she's tall and has strong legs. You're saying that's not racial?'

'She's Tutsi, it's true. But her great-grandfather was Hutu. He was an intelligent man who inherited only four cows from his father but left sixty to his son. That's why they ended up calling him "Tutsi", because he became rich.'

'I don't understand why you married a Tutsi. You're an enemy of our people, an enemy of Rwanda.'

'I'm not an enemy of Rwanda. Hutu and Tutsi are brothers, just like my children are brothers.'

'Your children aren't brothers, they're Hutu, except for the last one, who has a mixture of Hutu and Tutsi blood. A Hutsi so to speak! And the one about to be born is another Hutsi.'

'You make me ashamed. This discrimination, this hatred of the Tutsis, this obsession with finding differences, all brings shame to our country. There are not two ethnicities in Rwanda, only one. We are all Rwandan.'

'If the Hutu have taken power, it's because the Tutsi monopolized it for centuries, with the support of the Belgians.'

'Well, it seems the whites have changed their tune and support Hutus these days. The whites have always been on whichever side benefits them.'

The argument ended badly, with the brother breaking a beer bottle on a wall. Later, in the middle of the night, Anastase's house was machine-gunned and a bullet hit Mamafis in the arm. The emotion brought on her labour and she came into my clinic over a month before she was due. The newborn weighed only two kilos, but I managed to save him, thanks to the milk of a neighbour who had also just given birth. Mamafis didn't have enough herself.

At the roadblocks they say that Anastase is a weak man, because he doesn't have the courage to cut down his wife and his two Hutsi children. They claim he only kills Tutsis at night, so that his wife isn't any the wiser.

On the evening of 11 April, Mamafis' cook comes to me in the bush and says that Madame has offered to hide my children at her home; Anastase will protect them. Isn't it too risky to go as far as Mamafis'? We would have to cross an almost completely open space.

'Impossible,' I say.

Two grenades explode fifty metres away, and my decision is upended. I hug Joseph.

'Yolande, may Imana protect you.'

'But what about you, Joseph?'

'Me? As long as they don't have you, they won't kill me. By protecting you I protect myself too. I'm not afraid.'

Joseph's courage surprises me. I know that my husband is not a brave man. I know that he's afraid of death.

Alone, I return to my children in their hiding place. Their expressions frighten me suddenly, especially Christian's. He's become so thin, and Sandrine has protruding red eyes. Nadine gets up and as her dress falls over her hips, she catches it with one hand.

I need to show I'm in charge. 'Follow me, no time for questions.'

'But why? Where are we going?'

'Be quiet, Nadine.'

Nadine falls down abruptly. 'I'm thirsty,' she pleads, holding her forehead.

Christian takes off through the bush. I don't dare call out to him. He enters a house occupied by Hutus and comes back carrying a large saucepan carefully.

'Here,' he says to his sister, 'drink. It's milk.'

He looks at me with pride. Nobody caught him stealing. My son knows what war is like. I'm proud of him.

The milk is boiling hot so we have to wait. Sandrine won't, she plunges her hands into the pan, cups the milk, then raises her hands, letting the milk pour back into the pan. 'This way, it will cool faster.'

'You're going to burn your hands,' I say.

'What does that matter? My sister is thirsty.'

I think of the saying: 'Tutsis, drinkers of milk.' I remember a story I was told as a child: 'Imana came down one evening to his favourite land, Rwanda. He offered a jug of milk to a Twa child, a Hutu man and an old Tutsi man. Then he went to rest on a hill. The next day, he returned. "What did you do with my milk?" he asked the Twa. The child explained that he knocked it over in his sleep. "And you, Hutu, tell me, where is the milk I gave to you yesterday?" "The milk? I drank it. I was thirsty." Imana turned to the old Tutsi man, who handed him the jug of milk. "You don't like the milk that I give you?" asked Imana, angrily. "Yes I do, my Lord. I love it so much that I would rather keep it for you and your return."'

Perhaps it's because of legends like this that the Hutu hate us.

Nadine only manages to wet her lips. She vomits immediately. We leave the saucepan in the bush. Maybe the birds, those sons of Imana, will come to quench their thirst.

Christian and Sandrine interlace their fingers to make a makeshift chair for a vanquished queen. Nadine sits on it and I lead us down a small path that winds its way between the houses. We pass through unnoticed and almost laugh with relief.

But then: a roadblock. I have just enough time to warn the children; we throw ourselves down and crawl away through the undergrowth. Did the two men smoking cannabis and drinking banana beer see us? They get up and come towards us, but don't seem to suspect anything. They're simply doing their rounds, their rifles still slung across their shoulders.

One of them says, 'I'm afraid of an ambush, let's go to the bar for backup. I'm sure there are cockroaches hiding here; I saw the grass move.'

A caterpillar crawls over Sandrine's leg, leaving one of its stinging bristles on her skin. She stops herself from screaming. With a flick, she sends it into the thickets. She removes the bristles and massages the spot. The two men move further away.

I fear they'll return with an army of Hutus, sweeping the bush with machetes. Fifty metres away, I can make out the chicken coop of some friendly Hutu neighbours. Well, at least they *were* friendly before Habyarimana was assassinated. Their house seems to be deserted, so I decide that we'll hide in their chicken coop. We reach it without mishap and night falls on us like a gesture of friendship. It's a small hut, two metres high, backing onto the hill. We slip through its small, low door; my girls crawling on their sides so that their hips can pass. The chickens cluck for a while, as if to celebrate our arrival. Christian tries to caress them to quieten them down. In the dark we touch each other to be sure we're all there. My beautiful family holed up in a chicken coop! I think of Joseph, who must be at the roadblock at this moment.

We hear men's voices admonishing each other. They're looking for us. One even calls out: 'Muganga! Muganga! We know you're out there. If you give yourself up, we'll spare your children.'

The shout chills me. Am I endangering my children by hiding myself? I feel a peculiar love for this stranger who shouts in the night that he will save my children. I want to give myself up.

'It's a trick, Mama,' says Christian. 'Don't go. They'll kill you, and afterwards they'll kill us too.'

I obey. I obey my son; I'm not sure why. Christian must be right; we're not in a place where men can be held to their word. But what if this man is speaking the truth? No, he's lying. Unless... I don't give myself up, not so much because I make a decision, but so as not to disobey Christian.

Sandrine's breathing turns to panting. I grope my way towards her. A chicken that I've upset begins to beat her wings vigorously. 'Be quiet, you beast!'

My daughter is suffocating. It seems like an asthma attack. I listen carefully. No, it's an allergic reaction. I pull her towards the door of the chicken coop, put her head outside. She takes three big breaths. 'Mama, look at the stars. They're so beautiful!'

'Yes, yes,' I say to cut short the conversation. 'Now, come back in.'

As Sandrine slides back inside, her tall body frightens me. She's no longer a child: she's a woman.

Gunshots in the distance. Is that Joseph's death that I've just heard?

'I'm thirsty,' Nadine says.

I slide out of the chicken coop with difficulty and look around, groping hopefully for the chickens' water bowl. My hands discover something plastic, and I feel it over, trying to make out what it is. A jerry can! 'Water! Water!' I shout, forgetting the danger.

I crawl back quickly into the coop and with my fingers search for Nadine's mouth and slide them between her teeth. I tip the jerry can, and hear the sound of her swallowing. She coughs.

'A drink! It's so long since I last drank water.'

We all drink after Nadine. We don't know whether it's drinking water, but we don't care after a whole day without a single drop. Water gives us back a feeling of serenity and we sleep like logs.

I'm woken by the neighbours' return in the morning. By their own account, they've 'worked' hard all night. A man with a deep voice boasts about having cut off two heads. Another, with a clear, resonant voice, asks to be allowed to cut off a head all by himself the following night.

'Tomorrow night, I'll make a man out of you. You'll have your cockroach, I promise you.'

As they chat, they walk around the chicken coop, swearing a little; they must be looking for the jerry can. Finally, they find a pitcher and use it to pour some water into a bowl for the chickens before leaving.

I wake up the children. 'We need to leave,' I whisper. 'It's too dangerous here.'

How to flee without crossing the garden? The children climb on my back, my shoulders, and then haul themselves up onto the roof of the chicken coop, which is level with the hill. They pull me up and we take off. We reach two houses occupied by Hutus, stop and hide. Christian spies on their movements in the living room. As soon as the occupants sit down, he will give us a sign. We wait for half an hour. Finally he signals and we make a dash for it, running up the hill to our house, Christian bringing up the rear. Joseph sees us, comes and hugs us for a long moment.

My sister Hilde arrives almost immediately, passing through the fence we broke through on the first day of hiding. She pushes a seven-year-old child in front of her. He says he has been sent by his father to tell us that I am the first on the list of people to be killed.

'Who is your father?'

'Have mercy!' says the child, terrified. 'Papa said I was not to tell you his name. You must hide yourselves.'

Gunshots ring out in the still cool air of the morning.

The child disappears into the bush, more agile than an antelope.

We don't so much as jump, as if resigned to our fate. We decide to return to our first hiding place in the bush. I tip a third of an enormous packet of sugar into a scarf, and each child fills two empty Fanta bottles with drinking water. Joseph carries a couple of eggs in each hand.

A plume of smoke, almost white, rises up about five hundred metres away, in the direction of my clinic. Another child appears. This one I know well; he lives close to my work.

'Muganga, they've broken down the door to the clinic with guns and looted everything: the machines, the microscopes, the medicines. I took the telephone to bring it to you.'

I look at him. Children have become the last messengers in this world of the deaf. I cry and hug the child, but I can't remember his name.

'They also burnt all of your books. They made a big pile of them in the garden, threw on some petrol and set it alight.'

Idiots. They could have used the medical books: *Tropical Pathology*, *Surgical Pathology*, *Obstetrics* and more. *Ngucire umugani* as well, a book of Rwandan legends. All that up in smoke!

I see two women on the road carrying bags of stolen medicines. One of them shows the other a package of a dozen bottles of cough syrup.

'These are for treating malaria.'

'Really?' replies the other woman. 'Ah! I thought they were for preventing malaria!'

We hear shouts from the roadblock – it sounds like a man being tortured. We need to go. Joseph doesn't want to hide any more, but I convince him to stay with us and we head further into the bush. Christian sets off first, as if he is the head of the family, moving fifty metres ahead of us, then making signs for us to follow him. In the bush, his expansive yet nervous gestures make him look like a police officer at a city crossroads.

It's beginning to get hot.

# 6

The Rwandan sun warms the heart as well as the body. It's never too hot – the wind sees to that.

A man is walking through the bush, heading directly towards us. The first thing I notice are the flaps on each shoulder of his shirt. He is small, even puny, and has on the black, blue and green beret of the PSD, the moderate Social Democratic Party. My husband is also a member. He's zipped up his navy jacket halfway and rolled up the sleeves. Underneath is a red T-shirt bearing four black letters that I can't read. Five grenades adorn his body: two hang by their levers from his pockets, three more from his belt. As he approaches, his jeans and dirty trainers become visible through the grass. In one hand, he is carrying a machete, and in the other another grenade, the pin ready to be pulled.

He moves straight towards Nadine, has he spotted her? I see the grenades up close: olive-green fruit, grainy like small avocados, decorated with a copper ring. The head of the detonator catches the light, silvery, like brushed aluminium. His machete shines. It's brand new, perhaps one of those bought recently by Habyarimana's regime with money from the French government, and distributed free of charge to the Hutu population. It's a butcher's knife, sixty or seventy centimetres long, curved at one end and set at the other between two rounded pieces of wood riveted together to serve as a handle. The sharp edge is convex, the opposite of the concave curve of a sickle.

The man glances around as though he's hallucinating or drunk. His eyes are red, his nose narrow like that of the 'typical' Tutsi. He seems to be more afraid of himself than of anyone else. 'Where is your father?'

He has seen Nadine. She doesn't reply.

'Don't be afraid. I'm not here to harm him.'

She lowers her head and her eyes seek me out. Luckily, the man doesn't notice.

'André, I'm here. Why are you looking for me?' Joseph reveals himself.

André sobs, 'Listen carefully, Joseph.' He is dripping with sweat while my husband remains calm. 'You're my neighbour and I've got nothing against you or your family, but we've been ordered to exterminate all Tutsis without exception. Friends and relatives, adults and children. Listen to the radio: it's an official order. You want to know why I'm looking for you? I'll tell you. I've been ordered to set the bush on fire, because everyone is convinced you're hiding here. I've come to warn you, get out of here! Go to my grandmother, I know she likes you a lot. But beware of my father, he's a cruel and ruthless man. Please don't tell him I'm the one who told you to hide there. Go! I'm setting the bush on fire right away to show I'm obeying orders and to protect all of us. Take that path just a bit further down, there aren't any checkpoints and you'll only be out in the open for two or three minutes. Take your family and leave! I'll pretend I haven't spoken to anyone. I'm going to walk around the base of the hill; when I come back you must be gone. If I have any advice for you, it's to go to your assigned roadblock because people are saying you don't go often enough, they say you're abandoning your country to the rebels.'

André moves away, his grenades knocking together.

Joseph turns towards me. His face is almost grey, his eyes bulging.

'You know this man?'

'Yes. He's the district's Social Democratic Party representative. I met him at the meetings. What a change! A month ago he was a smiling boy, now he's someone else. Did you see how afraid he is?'

André has disappeared into the valley. Joseph can't bring himself to return to the roadblock. Trembling, he decides to come with us: a huge risk.

We set off to Mukecuru's house – Grandma, as we call her, out of respect. Joseph scrambles after us: his survival depends on nobody suspecting that we're together. For fifty metres, we're hidden by tall grass. When we reach the low grass, we catch our breath under a shrub, then run with all we've got. We haven't covered thirty metres when a woman raises the alarm, ululating loudly. Immediately, three other women appear, uttering insults and calling the men at the roadblock. 'There are the snakes. Catch them!'

I recognize the voice of a woman I treated last week. Some adolescents take up the chase, running through the thickets. Someone throws a grenade but it explodes just short of us.

We slide into a long gulley that runs parallel to the slope, almost a ditch. We wait there briefly for Joseph and then continue along with the children in front. We're about thirty metres away from Mukecuru's house, hidden behind a rubber-hedge euphorbia, when boys armed with home-made clubs reach the place we were a few minutes earlier. They look like fools, searching for our tracks lower down in the valley. Amongst them is a child, six or so, with an amputated leg, hopping along on crutches. I see another boy I saved from malaria not too long ago.

I feel betrayed by those I helped. Was I a fool? What did I do to Imana that we should be hounded like this? I want to cry but no tears come. I force myself to smile; the children shouldn't see me crying. I notice a string of banana fibre in the hedge, detach it patiently and slide it through the hooks on my waistband. Don't we say iyo udafite umukandara ukenyeza umugozi – if you don't have a belt, use a string? Make do with what you have. The plumpness that once held up my jeans has deserted me.

Shrill whistles. One long sound followed by two short, then someone responds, in the distance, with three short whistles. Whatever they mean, we have no other options, so we rush to Mukecuru's house.

Mukecuru is a dishevelled little old lady. She's wearing a many-coloured cloth, a long red skirt and a brownish T-shirt. Her feet are bare, with dirt between her toes. She cries when she sees us and hides us straight away in a tiny windowless room that we cram into as best we can. We hear her pushing a sorghum grinder in front of the door with all her meagre strength. The weight of this pair of stones, one large and hollowed out, the other an oblong pestle, will surely dissuade the murderers from looking any further.

Almost immediately, the Interahamwe arrive and search the house.

'Are you sure they didn't get in without you knowing?'

Mukecuru replies with poise: 'Absolutely sure. I was sitting right there at the door where you found me. But if I see them, I'll give one long and two short whistles.'

'How good you are, Mukecuru. The Hutus will know how to thank you!'

We spend all day in this dark room, speaking in whispers, my family reunited. Nadine moans a little, she's thirsty. A banana leaf slid under the door makes us jump. I bend over to smell it. Boiled rice! 'Thank you, Mukecuru.'

'Quiet, you're going to give yourself away!'

Other leaves follow. More rice, crushed broad beans, and finally some water that Mukecuru pours under the door, and that we suck up from the smooth earth floor on our hands and knees.

'Silence, you thirsty lot!'

Around midnight, we hear a man whining, asking questions. It must be André's father. Why has Mukecuru moved the sorghum grinder? To clean the kitchen, she says. To clean? But she hasn't cleaned anything. It's true, she says, she was interrupted by the Interahamwe who came to interrogate her for ages about the people they said had passed by her house.

Two hours later we recognize André's voice. His father shouts at him, blames and insults him. 'What? You've been through all the bush and you haven't found them!'

'I don't know how they escaped, Father. They're so cunning.'

'And you, you're stupid. They must have played tricks on you and you believed them. I must have Muganga, I must! They've promised that whoever finds Muganga won't have any more problems. Who were you talking to in the bush this morning?'

'A militia man who was lying in wait for them.'

'What was his name?'

'I don't know. I didn't know him.'

'I'm telling you, that militia man will end up finding Muganga before me, and then I'll look like a fool because I promised *I* would catch her.'

The conversation breaks off, interrupted by whistles in the distance. I'm exhausted and begin to drift off to sleep.

All of a sudden, someone kicks the door in and light dazzles my eyes. A small man stands in front of me and shouts: 'I knew it! Since yesterday, I've had a feeling that you were hiding here! My son gave it away; he was sweating like a thief when I questioned him.'

'If you knew, why didn't you kill me yesterday?'

My calm throws him off-balance. He hesitates, then says: 'It's because I like you a lot, Yolande. I didn't want to hurt you, but I am obliged to kill you.'

Mukecuru intervenes. 'If you shed a drop of Tutsi blood, may that blood haunt you and your descendants. I am your mother, Jean, don't forget.'

'I don't care! All I want is for them to leave.'

He grasps me with a weak hand. I resist, get up and tower over him. 'If you want to kill me, go ahead. You have a machete in your hand. Kill me and kill my children too.'

My ruse saves our lives. Jean throws us out, but shows us a path that will lead straight to our house without being seen. He is a fanatic who knows how to hate but doesn't know how to kill. Or is he heading to our house to kill us without his mother knowing? The genocide has started to exude its poison into our bodies, affecting every organ. Families are tearing apart; sons no longer respect their mothers; brothers no longer respect their sisters; and he who loved his fellow man now has a heart of stone.

# 7

**W**ater runs the length of my body. I gulp down mouthfuls from the shower. I'm a free woman, I can wash myself. Free, but only to wash myself. Anything could happen next. In a few minutes Jean might arrive with the Interahamwe and drag me naked from the shower. If I must die, may I at least die clean.

But I'm afraid to stay too long in the bathroom. I feel vulnerable naked; I'm resigned to death but not to being raped. If the Interahamwe find me dressed perhaps I'll be spared that humiliation. But if I am to be raped, may it be by the unhappiest of Hutus; he who hasn't yet known love. That would be my last gift. I must be going mad; I no longer even know what I'm thinking.

I like our shower; it was our second bed. Joseph and I would enjoy finding each other there in the morning. Sometimes I decorated it with flowers and we'd look at ourselves together in the large mirror. The children asked why our showers lasted so long and we explained that being larger than them, we had more surfaces to wash.

This morning, the mirror reflects a faded flower: my body. I call Joseph and he comes running. 'Look at these spots on my arms. There's nothing left of my buttocks. And my thighs: I've become an old woman!'

Water runs along my stretch marks, they've turned into deep cracks like those of a dry river bed. Joseph looks at me without desire. 'What are you thinking about?' he says.

'I'm thinking about this shower. About love. I'm thinking...' I don't dare finish my sentence. 'And you, what's on your mind?'

'That everything is over. It's the thirteenth, Yolande.'

Joseph is not normally superstitious. And yet, goose bumps now cover his body and he shivers. 'I've washed too,' he says, as if I didn't know.

I understand from his eyes what he wants to say. That the showers we've taken this morning, one after the other, are a form of purification, perhaps our last showers before death.

Joseph hands me a large bath towel in the colours of the Rwandan flag, embellished with a black gorilla in the place of the R. This towel was a present from José, a Belgian zoologist my niece does the housekeeping for in Kigali. Belgians have fallen out of favour so his life is also in danger. I dry myself with an almost sensual pleasure and then sit down on a little bench, wrapped up warmly in my national flag.

Joseph sits beside me and takes my hand: 'Dear, Yolande. Please forgive me for not listening to you before. I have a feeling I'll be killed today. Stay as courageous as you've always been. I pray that you and the children survive. Thank you, Yolande, for having been everything to me: my mother, my sister and my wife all at once. Farewell. I'm going to the roadblock. Soon, this will all be over.'

We remain for a long time side by side, silent, overwhelmed, looking at the hill opposite us through the window.

Suddenly, he exclaims: 'Cyanika! If only I had died in Cyanika!'

Joseph has told me the story a thousand times. It starts on Christmas morning in 1963. He's thirteen. Men armed with machetes and clubs burst into his parents' house, tie up his father and eldest brother and take them away. Joseph will never see them again. The men come back and take the girls, leaving Joseph and his mother alone. She dresses him in girls' clothing and sends him off to the house of his godfather, who hides him in a large basket of beans for three days. The same armed men arrive and search the house but they don't find Joseph. They swear and slap the godfather, they know a young boy has escaped their grasp. The godfather pretends he doesn't know a thing. That afternoon, he takes Joseph to say goodbye to his mother.

'Why goodbye?' asks Joseph. 'I don't want to say goodbye, I want to stay with Mama.'

They find the house, Joseph's childhood home, consumed by flames. Someone is calling from the inside: Joseph's mother. The godfather goes into the flames and pulls her out by her feet. She is burnt all over, but still, she calls to her son, holds out a clenched fist, and says: 'Take it, take it!' But she doesn't have the strength to open her charred hand. She faints. No, she is dead. Joseph unfolds his mother's fingers one by one. They are hiding a twenty-franc note.

The godfather finds a dozen charred bodies: Joseph's aunts and cousins.

The child returns to his godfather's and the next day he sends him to the parish of Cyanika, where Tutsis are hiding. 'Go, go,' says the godfather, frantic. 'They'll come back here for sure. Avoid the main roads.'

Joseph hugs his godfather goodbye and leaves before daylight, still wearing a little white dress and blue headscarf tied at the nape of his neck like a country girl. He has seven kilometres to cover on foot. When he hears men's voices, he hides in the bush. He gets to a wooden bridge held up by creepers that crosses the Mwogo River. He sees no one, so he starts to cross. Behind him, three men jump out of the bush and chase him, the bridge shaking under their feet. Joseph is paralyzed by fear and they catch him.

'Hold her,' one of them says, 'I've heard that raping a young girl is excellent medicine for my illness.' With one hand he unbuttons himself, with the other he tears off the child's clothes and discovers that he's a boy. Shouting with rage, he picks Joseph up and throws him into the river. When the child comes to, he is lying on the grass, a woman kneeling beside him, wringing her wet clothes. Joseph tries to stand but fails, the woman wraps her cloth around his naked body and carries him away without saying a word. Joseph tells her he must go to the parish church.

'That's where I'm taking you,' she replies.

At the church entrance, Joseph hugs the woman who saved him. 'What is your name?' he asks her. The woman doesn't answer, she simply smiles and leaves.

Joseph spent several months moving from boarding school to orphanage, from orphanage to foster family, from foster family to boarding school, up until the day my mother's aunt adopted him. And that's how I met Joseph, when I was still a child.

A grenade explodes in the distance. Joseph's hand in mine doesn't so much as twitch. Explosions have become an everyday noise, like horns beeping in the National Unity Square during rush hour.

Throughout my childhood, Joseph was like a big brother to me. We played together until I was fifteen, when I learnt that he wasn't my cousin but an adopted orphan. At first, I pitied him. I saw him as a wounded young man, felt for him, and treated him kindly. In return, he became my confidant and gave me advice. I often told him about my romantic encounters with boys. He listened sweetly, but insisted that I was too young to get married; that I shouldn't pay too much attention to boys. One day, a few years later – I'm not quite sure how it happened – we got married. I was not in love with Joseph, but this didn't worry me. 'The fire that burns fiercely, goes out fast,' my parents had warned me. They said love should be a cooking pot that warms up slowly, with the soup becoming tasty only after hours of cooking. As I got to know Joseph better, I stopped pitying him and began to admire him. At the birth of Christian, I discovered a father in my husband. At the birth of Nadine, I fell in love. That's love in Rwanda.

As for our arguments, they were almost always about one thing: whether we should send our children out of the country for their safety. Joseph didn't want to, I did. 'To what end?'

Joseph would ask. 'To live in a refugee camp? And, if we're killed, they will be orphans just like I was!' Our discussions would go on for hours, sometimes turning into rows, but never reaching any decision. They invariably ended with Joseph offering to go if needs be, leaving me the house and the children. Sometimes we talked about divorce but never made up our minds. Actually, there was once when we did decide to get divorced. But it was a joke, I think.

'I'm going to leave,' said Joseph. 'But, when all's said and done, I like this house. What about if you left? Huh?'

'OK. Tomorrow, I'll leave.'

'Fine. But let's make love for the last time.'

'OK. We'll make love all night long, and tomorrow we'll get divorced.'

The next day, I got up in a good mood. 'Aren't we going to court?'

'To court?' Joseph was flabbergasted. 'But why?'

'To get divorced, of course!'

'Oh, right, I forgot.'

We kissed and never went to court.

We made love many more times, in the shower, in the dining room, the kitchen, the larder, and sometimes in the bedroom. 'In any case,' concluded Joseph proudly, 'your parents would never approve of a divorce, they know I'm the best man in the world.'

'I'm cold!' says Joseph.

His voice makes me jump, breaking the depths of my thoughts. I squeeze his hand.

'Goodbye,' he says, without turning away, his face still bathed in the early-morning light. We don't cry; we have no tears left. 'I'm going to the roadblock like everybody else. I can't fight it any longer. Forgive me, Yolande.'

'I don't need to forgive you,' I say calmly. 'It's not your fault or mine. Faced with death, we're beyond all blame. I love you, Joseph.'

'I'm proud of you, Yolande. Proud to have a wife who knows how to make peace... I've thought of a plan. It's safest if we all separate. I've already called your niece Spérancie to come and collect the children. You will hide in the bush alone.'

'But that's impossible,' I say, 'the children will have to cross the road and they'll be spotted by the roadblock guards.'

'I've thought of that,' replies Joseph calmly. 'I'll present myself at the roadblock as they cross; the Interahamwe will take their eyes off the road to focus on me.'

I'm surprised by Joseph's will, his courage, his ruse. It's as if, faced with death, he has become a stronger man. Even his tone is more authoritative.

Spérancie arrives and it's time for Joseph to leave. We hold each other and I murmur into his ear: 'I love you, Joseph.'

'I love you, Yolande.'

Joseph gets up. He seems almost serene, while I'm overwhelmed by grief. He speaks to Spérancie for a moment and I watch them, unable to move, unable to greet my niece. I can't take my eyes off my husband. He moves away quickly then turns for just a moment but I'm paralyzed, I can't even lift my arm to say goodbye. I look at him, stunned.

Joseph sets off for the roadblock, I lower my eyes, looking for tears I'll never find.

Spérancie comes to me, takes my hands. I say nothing.

I get dressed in jeans and a jumper, but I don't even know why. I look at the children, did Joseph bid them farewell? No, he didn't want to frighten them. They are sitting on the ground, so weak and thin. Now I know why I'm getting dressed: for them.

Joseph reappears. 'Quick, quick, they're coming! It's now or never: run, children. And you, Yolande, go hide yourself.'

He turns and goes back outside, faces his pursuer, a man with a machete glinting in the light. Joseph is using himself as bait to save the children. I'm proud of him.

Spérancie runs off towards the road with the children. My stomach is in tatters. No, I can't separate myself from them. I follow them, but they are already slipping into the grass on the other side of the road. I want to cross but whistles sound like thunderclaps. A neighbour has seen me, and alerts the Interahamwe with loud cries. Three militia men run towards me. I slide myself under a piece of sheet metal whose far side is hidden in the undergrowth. I edge my way along and fall a metre below into a path that I run down as fast as my legs will carry me.

There are cries in the distance: 'Muganga has hidden herself under this sheet metal. Get her.'

I smile. I cry for my children. I run. I see Côme's house and run towards it; perhaps they won't look for me there, since he's a Hutu.

# 8

'Is it really you, Yolande? You're still alive?'

Côme's wife, Cécile, looks at me, flabbergasted. She is tall and proud and must weigh at least a hundred kilos, which she carries with a certain grace. Little by little, her face changes, becomes wary, then mean. We're close neighbours, separated only by a house and a cowshed and yet she doesn't like me, I'm not sure why.

'You haven't got a hope in hell,' she snaps.

'Who does, Cécile?'

'I don't know.'

'I do.'

'Who?'

'Those who kill.'

'Perhaps.'

'Can you hide me?'

My question makes her uncomfortable. She doesn't reply.

'Can you hide me?' I insist.

She relents feebly, half-heartedly: 'Not here.'

'Not here? Why not?' I say, forcing my way into the house.

There is an indecipherable silence between us.

From the road comes the dull rhythmic sound of people being hit with clubs. Out of the window, I see a group of seven or eight soldiers come round the bend, their black boots pounding the ground. At the front is a stocky militia man armed with a machete, his bottom sticking out as if he didn't have time to wipe after relieving himself. It's Côme! He's in charge of the roadblock! It dawns on me I've sought refuge with my enemies.

'But he's crazy,' I say. 'Your husband has gone crazy!'

'There was no other option,' Cécile responds. 'If he had refused they'd have killed him.'

'If he had refused, if he had refused... Look at him! He's proud to be hunting Tutsis!'

The group passes, heading to the roadblock where Joseph is now. I peer between the houses and the banana trees and hear orders: Hutus must stand on one side of the road, Tutsis on the other. I think I can make out Joseph, standing up straight, looking the soldiers in the eye.

They check identity cards. Côme is surprised to see Paddy, a dwarf, on the Hutu side. Snippets of what they say reach us.

'But Paddy, you're a Tutsi!'

'Not at all. I'm a Hutu.'

'But you've always said that you are Tutsi!'

'That was to make people believe I'd grow one day,' replies the dwarf.

'It doesn't matter whether you're Tutsi or Hutu,' one of the soldiers says. 'Paddy, we'll save your life today so that one day, when there isn't a single Tutsi left alive, you can tell people what they were like.'

There's a scuffle, I can't make out what's happening. I can't see Joseph any more. Gunfire bursts through the air, bodies fall on the road and the assembled Hutus look on with fear. The soldiers regroup and set off in step towards the next roadblock. A man runs for a moment, then collapses.

My head spins, I fall and throw up.

Struggling to my feet again, I look out of the window, dazed. People are looting our house, making off with my fridge, my bed, my radio and my telephone. My life is falling apart, my husband is dead, I no longer have a home. But at least my children are still alive. I want to join them.

A silhouette staggers towards our house. It's Joseph! His shoulder is bleeding copiously. I want to cry out, but I hold myself back just in time, gesticulate instead, but he doesn't look my way. He disappears inside.

A voice behind me makes me jump. It's Côme. He is right there in front of me: foolish, ugly, squat, hypocritical. How else can I describe him? In his arms, he's holding clothes that belong to my husband: two pairs of trousers, a few shirts, a pair of shoes and three suits. Behind him, two teenagers carry my cooker, with a sack of sugar, slashed open and squashed into the oven.

Côme, embarrassed, pretends to cry. 'The soldiers looted your house and I wanted to save what I could to give it back to you.' He holds out Joseph's clothes towards me.

I'd never heard anyone lie with such impudence. A thought crosses my mind, perhaps he doesn't know that Joseph is still alive?

'Keep them,' I say, 'I no longer have any use for them. Joseph is dead. He's just been killed. Keep Joseph's clothes for yourself and give everything else to your wife.'

I see the satisfaction in his eyes and a wave of contempt washes over me; I want to spit in his face. He and his wife go into their bedroom and talk in low voices for a while. Sugar crunches under my feet as I move towards the cooker. I take a bowl and use it to transfer what remains into my pockets. Imagine having to steal my own sugar, I think sadly.

Côme reappears. He seems furious. He says to my face: 'You cannot stay here; it's out of the question. The soldiers think we're hiding Tutsis and they're going to start searching house to house, starting with mine. If they find you here, they'll kill me and my wife. You have to go.'

He hardly dares look at me; it's as if he's talking to the table and chairs. He must be lying. I lay a trap. 'Tell me where to hide then?'

He smiles faintly, relieved. 'In the plantation. Come, I'll make a hole in the fence for you.'

I follow him, and disappear amongst the plants without thanking him.

These are tall plants, fodder for animals. But there are no more animals; they've been killed. Their mistake? Belonging to

Tutsis. As I make my way through, the plants move, betraying my whereabouts. I crawl along as delicately as possible.

The plantation is as crowded as the market in Kigali. There are so many Tutsi hiding here that we almost bump into each other. I pass by Théophile, whose pregnant wife was raped after the killings started. The assailants slashed her open to see what a Tutsi baby looks like in its mother's stomach. They also cut the tendons on her feet. She died, at last, when someone put a bullet in her head. Théophile and I look at each other, tears in our eyes, talking without words, then continue on in search of shelter. I pass other fugitives, a pretty girl around twenty years old, a distant cousin, a seminarist, a Toyota garage owner. I decide to crawl to the end of the plantation and then walk back along the edge so that I can hide against the fence at the end of Côme's garden. Soon, three Interahamwe, alerted by Côme no doubt, begin working their way through the plantation with great machete blows. I can't see much from where I'm hiding but I hear a male voice begging for mercy followed by a gunshot.

The Interahamwe leave the plantation so I head back there right away, slipping between two of them as they march in parallel lines twenty metres away from each other. They circle Côme's house, certain that I must have hidden myself in his garden. Yet again, it's not my time to die.

I stay on the ground for a good while, then, seeing that the Interahamwe have gone, stealthily draw closer to the road block. Three men in helmets, two with machetes and the third with a club covered in nails, are beating someone up as if he were a sack of potatoes. They pull him up: it's Joseph.

'You snake,' cries one. 'Where is Muganga? Eh! Whether you answer my question or not, your time has come.'

Another shouts: 'All of Kigali knows that your wife is Dallaire's mistress. They said so on the radio.'

Why this obsession with Dallaire?

I see Joseph's hand fall onto the road, cut clean off with a machete. A red veil slides in front of my eyes, I feel like I'm suffocating, I faint.

It's dark when I come to. I'm cold, terribly cold. And parched. I see Joseph's hand falling once more. Blood beats in my ears and I think I'm going to faint again. I hear moaning in the distance. It seems to be coming from another roadblock. 'Kill me, kill me, for pity's sake!' someone cries.

I pull myself up a little, and in the dark, make out a man sprawled on the road, doubled over with pain. Men walk past with machetes, not paying him any attention.

As if I've had enough of living, I return to Côme's house. I find a kennel in the garden and slip inside. Rain has leaked through the dilapidated roof, filling an abandoned bowl. I gulp it down, but it's barely a mouthful. Once again, I risk everything and enter the house. I'm simply too thirsty. Again, Cécile stares at me with shock and disbelief.

'I must be immortal!' I tell her with pride, to underline her husband's incompetence. 'Have you heard anything about my children?'

Cécile tells me they're still alive. They were held at the roadblock with Spérancie but were let go. Cécile's expression is malicious; is she lying to me? Are my children dead? No, if Cécile wanted to hurt me, she would have said they were dead.

I order her: 'Give me some water!'

'Water?'

'Yes, water. Clear water. Preferably liquid,' I mock her.

As she goes to draw water from the rainwater tank, I take the opportunity to empty her sugar bowl into my jeans pocket. She returns with a miserable little cup that I swallow in one gulp. I hate her for not giving me a pitcher filled to the brim.

'More!' I beg, pretending to be more exhausted than I am.

She brings me some more and I gulp it down. I feel my stomach swelling. I hope she'll offer me something to eat.

'Would you like to eat a little? I've got broad beans.'

I force a warm smile and accept. They are large red broad beans flavoured with ginger. I eat slowly, but after about four, I can't swallow any more.

I turn to her with calculated coldness. 'Your husband had better not play any more nasty tricks on me. He won't gain anything from killing me, but it will add to his list of crimes. If he doesn't kill me, others will. I can't escape and I know it. Don't spare me for my sake, but out of respect for yourselves. And watch out: I'm so despairing I could do anything.'

Cécile looks at me with bulging eyes. She stammers that she doesn't understand what I'm trying to say and doesn't want to make trouble. I understand enough for the both of us. I want her to believe she can take advantage of me, so that when Côme, with his usual hypocrisy, proposes another hiding place that he intends to disclose to the Interahamwe, I'll pretend to accept, then will go hide elsewhere.

When Côme returns in the middle of the night, he is stunned to find me there.

'Thank you, Côme, for allowing me to hide in the plantation. It's because of you that I'm still alive.'

Troubled, his face turns an almost metallic grey. 'You... Would you like a bedroom for the night?' he asks, trembling.

'No, I'm not sleepy. I'll just stay here in your sitting room.'

It amuses me to see him so fearful. If the Interahamwe arrive, no doubt he'll be executed with me. 'You seem to be afraid,' I say, twisting the knife in the wound.

'Me, afraid? Never. Why would I be afraid? Kigali airport has fallen to the Blue Berets. The rebels can no longer win the war.' He grins maliciously. 'You seem taken aback.'

I smile and we don't exchange another word.

Finally, Côme goes to his bedroom to lie down next to his enormous Cécile. I pace up and down all night. I hear them turning over twenty odd times in their bed. I'm pleased to hear them complaining about not being able to sleep. From time to time they turn on the radio, keeping it down low so I can't hear the news. Before the sun rises, Côme returns to the living room. He says he's seen soldiers searching a neighbouring house out of his bedroom window. He addresses me formally, almost solemnly: 'Madam, this must stop. I can't do anything to save you. I've heard on the radio that they're no longer killing women and children. So I'm asking you to leave.'

'Very well. In that case, take me to the house near mine where Tutsi women and children have sought refuge.'

'But how? The Interahamwe will see us—'

'You can say I'm your wife.'

'No, it's impossible.'

'No? In that case I'll call out to the Interahamwe and say you're hiding me.'

Beaten, Côme obeys. We go out in silence and walk down the road. Torch lights are moving around the neighbour's garden, most likely the Interahamwe are searching the grounds.

A voice addresses us sharply: 'Hey! Who goes there?'

'It's me, Côme, the roadblock guard. I'm with my wife. We're going to work to chase the snakes.'

'That's good, go ahead.'

Côme trembles with fear and picks up the pace, pushing me along. We pass a man moaning in agony, abandoned on the road since the previous day. 'Kill me, kill me, I can't take any more. Have pity on me and finish me off.' He has only one arm left, his intestines spill out of a large gash across his stomach like a greyish mousse, and his Achilles tendons have been cut.

'Kill him, Côme, since you're so manly.'

Côme refuses. He doesn't have the courage to kill, for good or for evil.

'Give me your machete then, I'll finish him off myself.'

'Give you my machete? So that you can kill me?'

'Kill you?' I say, 'I wouldn't dare.'

I mock him, but realize I don't have the courage to finish off this dying man either. For the first time since the assassination of President Habyarimana, it seems to me that the victim is no less of a coward than his executioner. What would I do if I had to kill or be killed? Right now, our executioners are victims too. But if they're victims, why do they torture first? Why this taste for blood?

We reach the house filled with Tutsi women and children. Côme pushes the branches of the hedge apart so that I can pass through, and then runs back home. I edge through the hedge, cross the garden and cross back through the hedge a little ahead, until I'm only fifty metres away from Spérancie's house where my children are supposed to be hiding.

In the distance I hear the Interahamwe running. Côme has betrayed me, of course. He shows them the place in the hedge where he supposedly saw me pass through. They search the garden, cursing the elusive Muganga. And yet I'm just a few metres away from them, on the other side of the fence.

'I want to kill her myself!' Côme says excitedly.

There is passion in his voice. It's not me he wants to kill. It's to kill. It's to spill human blood. With people watching. But he'd rather not see the eyes of his victim, he wouldn't be able to bear it, he wouldn't have the strength to kill. That's perhaps why he only works at night.

Côme is someone who boasts about killing Tutsis. He alerted the Interahamwe to make them believe that he wanted to kill me, but he doesn't have the guts. At least that's what I tell myself.

# 9

find my children wounded, but alive. Tortured and
humiliated, but alive. I tremble as they come towards me,
three small wise men in rags. We hug each other and cry.

Spérancie is sobbing in a corner of the room.
Emotionally exhausted, she can't take it anymore. She gets
up and disappears into the garden, leaving us to our painful
intimacy.

I discover I can still cry. But am I crying for my wounded
children, or because of the cowardice of men? The cowardice
of men like Côme. The cowardice of the international
community who have abandoned us, hampering the advance
of the rebel forces and preferring to support the genocidal
regime to the end.

'Kigali airport is in the hands of MINUAR. We don't
stand a chance.'

My children don't understand.

'What are you talking about, Mama? What is MINUAR?'

I crumple down in despair. How to explain to my already
traumatized children that the governments of Europe and
America are propping up this government, even though
they're aware there's a genocide going on? Uwasuze agirwa no
kunutsa: if you pass wind in public it might as well smell bad.
I no longer know what to think or what I'm saying. Am I going
mad? I've hardly eaten for a week. Then Nadine hugs me, and
I feel like I'm waking up from a nightmare. My children, so
you're here, still alive? I feel a burst of joy.

'What happened to you?'

Christian solemnly explains that they were summoned to the roadblock and the Interahamwe showed them the body of a dead man. He bursts into tears.

'They made us identify him. "Do you recognize this man? Do you?" shouted an Interahamwe. "He's a soldier from the Patriotic Front, isn't he?" It was Papa. His hand had been cut off and his face bruised. "That's not a soldier," I said, "that's my father."Then they started beating me. One of them struck me with his machete. I raised my arm to protect my neck and it broke under the blow.'

I examine his arm: an open fracture of the humerus. It needs care.

'Leave it, Mama. What's the point? They said they'd come back tomorrow morning to kill us.'

I look at my son. In seven days he has been forced to become a man. I'm choked with pride and sorrow.

'We were surrounded by Papa's friends, but not one of them spoke up to correct the lie that Papa was a rebel soldier. If I could have...'

Christian falls silent, reflective. He really is a man now. He's beginning to have regrets.

He continues. Another soldier reprimanded the one who tried to cut his neck, saying that the children were to be killed only after revealing where their mother was hiding. The Interahamwe interrogated them one by one, but got nothing.

'They were crazy, Mama. They hit Nadine on her legs for what they called her "long Tutsi legs". They mocked Sandrine, saying that she was trying to grow as tall as the trees. They made us repeat after them that you are a captain in the Patriotic Front, and the mistress of someone called Dallaire. That this Dallaire rescued you by helicopter and you abandoned your own children. They made each of us repeat all of their lies. Then they turned on Spérancie, scratching and slapping her, spitting in her face. "Where is Muganga? Where is Muganga?" Spérancie said you must have been killed since she hadn't seen you for two days. "You're lying, witch!" And they beat her again.'

My head spins. How can people have been manipulated to this extent?

Nadine huddles up against me. Tattered pieces of skin hang like worn flags from her bleeding limbs. Christian's head falls into my lap and Sandrine puts her arm around my shoulders. I'm receiving more from my children than I've been able to give them in fifteen years. I remember pictures of the Virgin Mary with her suffering son. I have not one but three children in pain.

Spérancie appears with a large basket on her head. She managed to buy mangoes from a neighbour.

'Eat,' she says to me. 'You must regain your strength.'

I look at the basket of mangoes listlessly; I'm not hungry.

Spérancie has a large bruise on her forehead; it's my fault she was beaten, she was beaten for looking after my children. She joins us on the floor, crying again. I remain with my children held close, caressing their heads for I don't know how long, as grenades explode from time to time in the distance. We don't have any energy left to say more, to go over the details of the brutality they've gone through. I don't want to tell them about my two nights on the run, nor how I saw Joseph die. We're quiet, we're together. Being together is the greatest gift I could receive this morning.

My mother sang me a song when I was a child:

*I loved my mother and I lost her.*
*I looked for my brothers and sisters, but couldn't find them.*
*I went to the neighbours, but they rejected me.*
*I am surrounded by my enemies*
*Like a tongue that slips between the teeth.*

The memory does me some good, but I don't have the will to sing the song to my children. Rwanda's troubles are on hold as our broken family comes together again. The crickets chirp, it's getting warmer outside. The smell of goat kebabs grilling on a neighbour's brazier wafts over. I'm hungry but I don't want to eat. I've been murdered from inside. I am Rwanda.

# 10

'**G**et out, snakes!'

My former gardener appears at a run, shouting himself hoarse at the end of the garden.

'Go! They'll kill you and your children with you!'

I look at him, stunned. He has a machete, he's a fanatic, so why doesn't he kill me? Is it because he doesn't have the courage, or because I once forgave him for stealing from me? Behind him, whistles, like the barking of a pack of dogs. We get up swiftly and Spérancie leads my children away behind a rubber-hedge euphorbia. I leap across the neighbour's garden. Nadine loops back to me for a hug, then runs off, almost happy.

I work my way along the hedge, crawling until I reach a neighbour's kitchen. I come face to face with my friend Déo, a small thin man I often lent things to: money, tapes of Brassens or Joe Dassin. He doesn't get on with his wife, Pauline, and often asks my advice about how to deal with her. It's mostly thanks to me that they're still together!

'Go away. Get out! Out of my house, snake!'

'But Déo –'

'I don't know you. Go on, go!'

'Déo, surely you're not going to abandon me –'

'Clear off or I'll denounce you,' he shouts.

The Interahamwe already surround Déo's fence, and are trying to force their way through. The whistles are driving me mad. As I run on towards the next house, a woman catches me.

'Muganga, is it you they're chasing like a thief, you who cured us all?'

Who is this plump little woman?

Her voice is plaintive. 'I'm Emmanuelle. Come.'

Is she mad? I don't know her. I don't remember treating her, yet she's going to help me. It's almost funny that this little round being, who drags her feet, is showing such courage.

Emmanuelle sublets a little house in Déo's garden. The Interahamwe are already searching the surroundings. She pulls me inside and pushes me into a wooden box. I fall like a dead leaf and feel charcoal pouring over me in the dark. Voices and whistles come closer. I feel a cold object slip into the hollow of my hip almost like a caress.

A man, drunk with anger, bays like a wolf: 'Where is Muganga? Where is Muganga?'

Emmanuelle replies with false eagerness, 'Over there by the banana plantation. I tried to stop her but she pushed me and hit my shoulder. Look!'

The man whistles, people charge through Emmanuelle's kitchen, shouting that this time Muganga won't escape them.

A hand rummages in the charcoal and takes me by the shoulder.

'It's me, Yolande. It's Emmanuelle. Don't be afraid, they've all gone. Come, I'll look after you. You're not hurt?'

'Hurt?'

'But the machetes?'

'What machetes? I didn't feel a thing.'

'What do you mean? They plunged their machetes into the charcoal three or four times.'

'Ah! Yes, something did brush past me for a second, but I thought it was you.'

'Lord!'

Emmanuelle falls to her knees and joins her hands together to pray.

I interrupt her. 'I must hide somewhere else,' I say, getting out of the chest. 'When they realise I've evaded them once again, they might come back here.'

I look around the place, examine the floor, the crevices in the wall. No, there's nowhere to hide. I notice a makeshift roof made from grey sheet metal, hanging from the outside wall and covering a concrete double sink. Under the sink, two sliding doors hide the pipework. I open them. A man springs out and straightens up.

'You're in more danger than me, Muganga,' he says. 'You hide here. I've been under the sink four days. It's not comfortable, but nobody has thought to check it for a Tutsi. Maybe they think it's too small a space. Go ahead, hide.'

At first, I refuse, but the young man bounds off towards another garden, so I lower myself under the sink as best I can. I have to put one leg on each side of the downpipe, curling up and bending my head to fit in. Patiently, with my fingertips, I succeed in sliding the doors closed. It's dark and I can barely move. Through a crack in the wood I see daylight and Déo's shadow as he passes in front of the sink.

'Emmanuelle,' he shouts, interrupting her prayers, 'if you're hiding Muganga, I'll denounce you at the roadblock.'

He orders her to empty the charcoal chest. She begs not to, saying it's too much work.

'Empty it or I'll kill you!'

She empties the chest. Déo is disappointed and leaves, swearing.

Emmanuelle places her cooker just in front of the sink doors.

'This way they won't suspect anyone is hiding here.'

I thank her.

'It's God you should thank. It's because I prayed that they didn't find you.'

In the distance the whistles start up again. They must have found someone else to chase. I think of my children; will they really spare them until they get their hands on me?

A round of gunfire, long, endless.

'Emmanuelle, tell me. Tell me they haven't just killed my children!'

No reply. She's gone out to see what is going on. I can only try to guess from the brouhaha of voices and a car beeping nervously as if it's making its way through a crowd.

My fingers search and grip onto objects: the groove for the sliding door, a piece of pipe. Where are my children?

After ten minutes or so, Emmanuelle returns.

'That wasn't your children being killed.'

I heave like a drowned man, saved just in time.

'It was your goddaughter, Eléonore.'

Oh, Eléonore. So beautiful and so clever. She was engaged to a Hutu neighbour who loved her like crazy. Their wedding was planned for May.

'But why did the gunfire go on for so long?'

Emmanuelle sighs; must she really recount it all? She must. The truth is always less painful than a lie.

Reluctantly Emmanuelle complies. Eléonore was undressed by the Interahamwe who wanted to rape her one by one before killing her. But at that moment, her fiancé appeared with a submachine gun and, in despair and rage, shot down Eléonore so that they couldn't touch her. An Interahamwe shot him down in turn, but his fingers gripped the trigger as he fell and bullets kept firing until the charger was empty.

The account cuts through my heart like a knife. Feeling sick, I ask Emmanuelle for a little water. She replies with three metallic taps on the cooker, our signal warning me that someone is approaching.

'Emmanuelle! Emmanuelle!'

'Télesphore? Are you crazy? You're going to be spotted. They're searching this whole area with a fine-tooth comb. Hide!'

'Emmanuelle, it's not worth it any more. Everything's over now. You're a good woman, that's why I've come to you. You know I'm being hunted everywhere and my wife and children have already been killed. I'm not fighting this; I'm going to the roadblock to give myself up. So I'm asking you to hear my will. I have a hundred thousand francs in my current account and the American Embassy owes me three months' salary. I should have received it on 11 April, only I haven't dared collect it. Here is a document authorizing you to manage my affairs. If I'm killed, give the money to my cousins in Kibuye. If you can't find them, keep it for yourself. Goodbye, Emmanuelle. And thank you for everything you've done for me.'

Emmanuelle tries to delay Télesphore, suggesting he eats something first.

'Eat? I haven't eaten in eight days. What does it matter?'

'I beg you, don't give up, Télesphore. All hope is not lost. Let's pray together.'

'Pray? What for? God won't hear us. It's been ten days since Imana last returned to Rwanda. Death, who has carried away so many, won't leave anyone behind.'

'Why think only of death? You must find hope – the example of Christ on the cross –'

'Didn't Christ say, "It is finished"?'

'If you go to the roadblock they'll kill you for sure. Ushaka urupfu asoma impyisi, he who seeks death, embraces the hyena. It's a suicide mission!'

'Let me go; I want to die.'

And with these words, I hear him leave.

Thirty seconds later there's another burst of whistles and cries. Men flood the compound, yelling like drunks. 'We know you're hiding Tutsis. We saw Télesphore leave your house just now.'

'I'm not hiding Tutsis,' replies Emmanuelle with a calm that I can't understand. 'Télesphore came to ask me to contact his mother in Kibuye, because he was going to give himself up at the roadblock and knew he'd be killed. I don't like Tutsis, but you can't refuse a man who is going to die such a favour.'

'You're lying! Télesphore's mother has been dead for two years!'

'Not at all,' retorts Emmanuelle with aplomb, 'it's his grandmother who died.'

'Yeah, right! Come on, let's search the house.'

They hurry into the kitchen making a terrible din. A shot rings out in the distance.

'One less snake to worry about,' says one of the men, laughing.

They look for me across the neighbourhood, all night long.

# 11

t's beginning to get light. I don't know how to escape death but at least I'm no longer afraid. Sooner or later surely they'll find me behind these pipes and drag me to the roadblock. How will they kill me? By gunshot? With a machete? For women, it's most often with a machete. At this point, I don't care. Let Mayimuna cut off my breasts if she wants to. Suffering? I don't think about it.

Perhaps because I'm in such an uncomfortable position, I feel a tearing sensation in my stomach as if I'm in labour. I think about my first birth, my son Christian, my beautiful eldest boy.

Disregarding the danger I'm in, as if I'm indifferent to the risk of being caught, I set out obsessively to remember his birth. I feel myself detaching from this world, like the saints who smile up at the sky while being killed; those saints depicted in the pious pastel-coloured pictures the missionaries showed us at school. I sing inside as I remember my son's arrival.

My world is no bigger than the base of a sink; Rwanda is outside, and I'm no longer a part of it. In this imaginary world, there are no more Hutu or Tutsi, no good or bad, no politics or religion. In this world, where I've just risen like the Virgin Mary at the Assumption, there's only a woman bringing forth a beautiful child, a child who no more wants to be born than he wants to die today. The labour is long. My son shows no desire to come out and see the world, just as I, aching, contorted and curled up under my dear sink, have no desire to leave and see what Rwanda is up to. Why doesn't the earth open and swallow me up in its depths forever?

Rwanda, if it still exists, is shouting itself hoarse, like a drunk being thrown out of a bar at night: cries, laughter, pleading, insults, whistles and barking. Rwanda is made up of six or seven men, two metres away from me, swearing that they'll find Muganga and cut off her breasts. A thin partition separates me from that Rwanda over there. The fact that they don't even think to slide open these doors makes me laugh at them silently. It almost brings me joy.

I hear Emmanuelle offering beer to the Interahamwe, and again I hold back my laughter. Beer at seven in the morning! They accept, freshen up at the sink and sit down on the floor. Two of them lean their backs against the doors to my hiding place. The wood creaks a little. I think I recognize the first cry of my son and I'm happy; I've given birth to my child for a second time. I've gone mad. I cry and laugh at the same time, in silence. Joseph bends over me, kisses me with passion. But no, it's the sink pressing against my cheek. My womb is empty and now I'm damp. A tiny leak in the pipe has wet my trousers. The coincidence amuses me.

I want to shout that I've performed a miracle: I've given birth to the same child twice. To announce to the murderers that death doesn't exist. Is Christian dead? Are all my children dead, while I'm still alive, under this sink, as if in the depths of the earth?

'Mayimuna says she's going to cut off her breasts and watch them fall like rotten mangoes.'

Smutty bursts of laughter. They're afraid of killing, they need to laugh. I listen to them complacently, drunk with joy and grief intertwined. My happiness is visceral, I'm so sad I feel like I'm about to have an orgasm of sorrow.

'We'll rape her. I bet she's got a wet pussy.'

'Dallaire will just have to share it with us!'

A spoilsport protests: 'Why should Muganga be raped? Why cut off her breasts?'

His words are met with a storm of insults. 'They said on the radio that she's a snake. And that she's Dallaire's mistress.'

'Because she seems to prefer white pricks,' adds another.
More laughter.

'Perhaps you're also a cockroach,' interrupts a serious voice. 'How old are you?'

'Sixteen.'

'Sixteen and you don't have a beard? Get over here, let me feel your chin. Eh! No beard at all. OK, I'll forgive you, because you're not a man yet. The growing child doesn't avenge his father. But you'd better understand that any Hutu who doesn't believe what is said on RTLM is a traitor. Apologize.'

The adolescent apologizes, acquiesces. Then goes even further: 'If I find Muganga, I'll cut her in two, like in the Bible.'

The men laugh at his naivety. Humiliation is what gives indoctrination its strength. Curiously, I feel I'm in a better position than this young man: at least I'm still master of my thoughts.

The conversation turns to bragging, cruelty replacing obscenity.

'I'd like to tie Muganga to a tree and have her watch as I cut off her children's arms before killing them.'

This knocks me sideways. Bile rises and I vomit in silence, it runs down my cheek and neck. I see Sandrine, her beautiful slender body that they said wanted to grow as tall as the trees. I see a machete, a field tool for cutting tufts of sorghum or pruning trees. A machete, pruning Sandrine! I conjure up the image as if this could prevent it from happening.

'One day, I will write all this down,' I vow to myself. 'May those who don't have the strength to read it denounce themselves as complicit in the genocide against the Tutsi in Rwanda. I, Yolande Mukagasana, declare before humanity that whoever doesn't want to know about the ordeal of the Rwandan people shares in the guilt of the perpetrators. The world will not cease to be violent if it doesn't examine its need for violence. I will write this not to scare you or make you feel sorry for me. I want to bear witness. These murderers here promise me the worst kind of suffering, but I neither hate nor despise them. I even feel sorry for them.'

Here is the paradox of the Christian West. Its symbolic figurehead, Christ, suffered what Rwandans are suffering today. How many pious images show Christ crowned with thorns, flogged, pierced with nails on his cross? How many Christians have looked at these painful images with fervour? And yet when thousands of Rwandans face similar suffering, the West's Christian eyes turn away with false modesty and pseudo-regret.

And soon, if the Patriotic Front wins the war, white legal advisors will come to try and defend those guilty of genocide. From here, underneath my sink, I can already see the lawyers filled with good intentions. Some will refuse to defend the accused, others will accept, if only to get a step ahead. I can already see Rwanda torn apart by the cowardly interests of outsiders. The intellectual elite will throw themselves at my destroyed country, mining it for fallacious arguments that serve fallacious causes. I hate the West. I hate civilized Western intellectuals. How many of them would be capable of saying what I utter now, under this sink: forgive them, for they know not what they do? That's the only phrase that remains from all my Christian education.

I think of Sandrine again, of her difficulties adapting to life with us after the death of her mother. She used to sit quietly by herself in a corner or play with the dog for hours. She came home from school with bad reports. But when she started boarding school, she finally understood that I loved her as much as my own children. When I visited her on Saturdays, she confided in me, sharing stories about the friends she'd made and the boys who had started to look at her. I see her, again, proud and calm, as she presented her school report card to me at the end of that year: she was top of her class. 'It's thanks to you, Mama,' she said.

The men on the other side of the doors are still talking as if they're in a bar. They have found a new topic to argue over: Habyarimana. For some, he's a great man because he prepared for the clearing away of the Tutsi. For others, he's a wimp because he didn't give the order to start work. He had to be killed for it to begin in earnest.

'It's his in-laws who were really in control,' someone throws out there.

'Reminds me of the old royal family – power struggles solved with bloodshed.'

'That's really like the Habyarimana family!' From my hiding place I'd like to add my own personal commentary: 'History always goes in circles.'

My mind moves to Nadine. But what can I say about Nadine? Between a mother and her daughter there's an intimacy that can't be explained. Men can't understand it: it's innate. I feel as if it's Nadine who's hiding under this sink, while I, I...

Where are my children? Are they still alive?

As if in response to my question, there are loud cries in the distance, muffled blows like stones falling in a pile, one on top of the other. The men get up and their voices drift away. Emmanuelle begins to sing. It's a code between us to say that there's no immediate danger. I listen to her lovely voice as she hums a song from my childhood, and the words come back to me:

'...*I went to the neighbours, but they rejected me.*

*I am surrounded by my enemies*

*Like a tongue that slips between the teeth.*'

Three metallic knocks on the cooker.

I hear Déo's voice: 'I beg you, Emmanuelle, if you're hiding Tutsis tell me. You know that I won't denounce them. But I don't want any trouble.'

'Tutsis?' says Emmanuelle with a note of disdain. 'The Interahamwe have searched this place from top to bottom; do you really think if I'm hiding any they wouldn't have found them? Do you think they're fools or something?'

'No, no, you're right. But promise me all the same that you will denounce Tutsis, or at least chase them away.'

'Promise me! Promise me!' She imitates Déo's sharp voice. 'This morning, Déo, you said you were going to kill me. Your word doesn't seem to mean much.'

More noises of falling stones reach my ears and Emmanuelle begins to sing again. Then once again, three metallic knocks. I listen but can't hear much; just the sound of sheet metal in the distance, being moved with a mighty din.

The entire day is punctuated by Emmanuelle's singing and her three taps on the cooker. At one point I hear a great commotion: people are carrying more sheet metal and throwing it down, one piece on top of another, with a noise like thunder.

I will soon have been under the sink for eleven hours. At that point I have no idea that I'll remain there for eleven days.

# 12

efore the President's plane was shot down, the Blue Berets drove around the roads of Nyamirambo, my home in the Kigali suburbs, daily. Children ran to see them pass by, waving, smiling, even singing. But the men from MINUAR continued without stopping, barely responding to the bounding children. Now all the white people have left the area, they've stopped driving through altogether. Nyamirambo has become a godforsaken place.

'The white man brought discord,' my father once said. 'He is intelligent but false. Try to get on with him, but never have faith in him. Never forget that the Belgians took the country and placed it into the hands of the Hutus.'

I remember my father returning from the centre of town in Butare with books on politics, newspapers, and new batteries for his radio.

'More paper?' My mother would cry. 'More money wasted on paper!'

What would my father think if he knew his daughter was hiding under a sink?

It's now totally dark. Emmanuelle still hasn't come to talk to me. Where is she? Without a signal from her, I don't dare move. I stay under my sink, the pipe's U-bend between my legs, my cheek pushed against the basin. The crickets have begun their nightly fanfare, so loud that I can't hear what's happening outside. But as long as the crickets are singing you know nobody is close, your enemy is not at your side.

Where are my children? Are they at least still alive?

At school the whites taught us that the Hutu was a man of the fields, happy with the fruit of the earth. The Tutsi, by contrast, came from Abyssinia, ancient Ethiopia, or even further away. From Tibet, some said. 'You just need to look at a Tutsi's noble profile to see his resemblance to an Ethiopian.' According to the Hamitic hypothesis, the Tutsis colonized the Hutus by offering them milk.

'That's not true,' shouted my father, when I told him what we had learned at school. 'The Tutsi is Rwandan. He speaks Kinyarwanda, just like the Hutu.'

I didn't know at the time that this so-called 'Hamitic hypothesis', once used by the whites to protect the Tutsis, would be exploited by the same whites to promote and control the Hutu revolution. But by the time Grégoire Kayibanda became President at Independence in 1962, we no longer believed in the Hutu revolution. All we knew was that he had united the Hutu vote by exploiting ethnic distinctions accentuated by the Belgians. We didn't see the evil coming. One year later, the first genocidal violence broke out, and Joseph lost his father, his mother, and all his siblings. That genocide was referred to by Western governments from Washington to Brussels as 'the usual tribal infighting'. But they were involved from the beginning: the masterminds of violence drew on UN Secretary-General U Thant's declaration in New York that the Rwandan people had the right to self-determination.

Today my world is no bigger than the space under a sink, my only inspiration is fear, my sole supporters the crickets outside. Didn't U Thant also feel alone? Did he not understand our fear? Was he lulled by the applause on the benches humming in his ears?

And now, in April 1994, while a genocide is taking place, while Tutsis are being killed, what is the United Nations doing apart from expressing platitudes but not acting, under the indecisive leadership of the current Secretary-General, Boutros Boutros-Ghali?

Who is barbaric now? Yes, cutting the arms off children with machetes, raping women before disembowelling them, leaving mutilated men to die in horrible pain on the side of the road, yes, all this is intolerable cruelty. But the West is cruel too. The West has left people to die of hunger again and again. With the Jewish genocide they refined cruelty to the utmost degree.

What right does the West have to judge that we're not worthy?

Am I not allowed to prefer seeing my children killed with a machete blow rather than having to imagine them dying of hunger in concentration camps?

I storm in secret under my sink.

The crickets go quiet, and in the distance, like background music, I hear intermittent bursts of gunfire. The quiet rhythm makes me think of birdsong. Then footsteps: someone is edging along the wall. He or she places a hand on the door of my hiding place, feels around, lifts up the handle and slides open the door.

'Pauline, what are you doing here? How did you know?'

'Don't say anything to Déo,' she says. 'He would kill me.'

She gives me a warm egg.

'Because you saved my daughter when she had rheumatic fever.'

'Do you know anything about my children?'

She shakes her head, and closes the door in silence. I don't know whether Pauline likes me. People say she's mean, but I find her mostly stupid. Her unusual generosity seems to be a way of letting me know that she's aware that I'm hiding on her property.

An egg! When did I last eat anything? Déo's wife bringing me an egg? How the tables have turned! I remember a conversation I had with her about condoms she'd seen in my clinic.

'You distribute those monstrous things?'

'Well yes, it's a Ministry of Health programme. I'm obliged to do so.'

'It's just another assault from those foreigners who think they know better than us. They want us to have fewer children, to depopulate Rwanda so that they can subjugate us more easily. And who knows whether these condoms are poisoned or not, huh?'

Pauline and her eight children. I smile remembering her fears. They remind me of a question I asked a Belgian doctor whose name I've forgotten: Why won't foreigners leave Africans alone to solve their own problems?

'Because they feel guilty, Yolande. They want to wash their hands of guilt by posing as the defenders of humanity. They think black people can't see the wood for the trees. Having made a mess, they play at being the doctors of the third world. You know, if I could, I would send all the foreigners away, myself included.'

I think of my grandfather and my great-grandfather, whom I was always told lived happily under their cow skins, leading their herds to pasture and smoking tobacco.

The crickets start up their racket again and I eat my egg. Ah, what pleasure! But the night is cold and I get desperate for Emmanuelle to come and see me. Gunshots continue and from time to time a grenade explodes. It must be past midnight. What if Emmanuelle has been captured and executed by mistake? What if Déo himself has betrayed her?

All of a sudden there are raised voices. Déo is hurling abuse at his wife, but I don't quite hear what he's saying. He seems very nervous.

Pauline shouts back: 'Now you're a murderer!'

'A murderer, me? I did what's just, that's all! I gave the snake what it deserved. I worked for my country, Rwanda. This country belongs to the Hutu. Those snakes want to steal everything, it's good we take back what is rightfully ours.'

Pauline cries, begging her husband to stop killing, but he gives her a slap and threatens to denounce her. The national poison has been introduced into homes. See how it stokes arguments between husband and wife.

They continue talking for a while. Then, through the crack in my door I see a beam of electric light sweeping Emmanuel's garden: Déo searching the compound for Tutsis once more.

Eventually, calm returns. Even the shots in the distance cease. The Hutu has had his fill of blood for today. The night can begin, three or four hours late. I pray for Emmanuelle, not to God, but to humanity. If she's dead, how will I get out of here? There's only one solution: to flee. But how will I know whether the Interahamwe are still on the lookout? I decide to leave when the stars pale. I cook up plans to reach the house of Belgian friends in the centre of Kigali. Two kilometres, mostly out in the open, with roadblocks every fifty metres! How will I get there?

Then I hear Emmanuelle singing softly. I can't believe my ears. I knock lightly on the door. It opens.

'Where are my children?'

Emmanuelle lowers her eyes.

'Yolande, Yolande, your children are dead!'

'What? It's not true! You're lying!'

'They are, Yolande.'

'No! I don't believe you! Did you see them die?'

'No.'

'I'm going to the roadblock!'

I've already crawled out from my hiding place.

'I'm going to the roadblock to tell them they're murderers. I'm going to tear out their eyes.'

'Yolande, calm down!'

'My children are dead and you want me to stay calm! Let me go!'

I struggle free from Emmanuelle's grip.

'Yolande!'

'What?'

'Yolande, I don't know. I'm not completely sure –'

'What?'

'I'm not completely sure they're dead. But that's what they're saying.'

I can breathe again. 'Where are they?'

'I don't know! All I know is that they've disappeared and Spérancie's house has been destroyed. Perhaps your children were able to flee, I don't know.'

I look at her intensely. Is she lying to protect me? No, I don't think so.

In silence I go to the toilet, and then come back and sit in her kitchen like a stone while Emmanuelle makes me some tea. I'm black with soot and dirt. There's a little egg yolk stuck on my shirt. I'm floating around in my jeans; I have to tighten the banana fibres that hold them up. I sit with my head in my hands, my elbows on the table, unable to speak. Little by little, though, I feel my body relax, and the aches ease.

We talk in low voices, keeping an ear out for any sound outside. Emmanuelle gives me the latest news. The new president has made a virulent speech against the Tutsi, congratulating soldiers for having taken the country's situation in hand, so that the majority can claim their rights. In Gitarama, Prime Minister Kambanda gave a tough-talking speech to soldiers, brandishing a revolver. Nobody should fear the ten per cent who humiliated the Hutu people in their legitimate development for centuries, he said. All you have to do now is set up roadblocks and catch them. He boasted about arms received from abroad: each Hutu will have his own weapon.

'And the RPF soldiers?' I asked.

'It seems they're close by, but nobody has seen them yet. Apparently the Hutus of Nyamirambo are lying in wait to ambush them, that's why they haven't yet dared approach. And the French continue to cross their arms courageously and do nothing. They say that in Kigali the Blue Berets are watching Hutus massacre Tutsis without even flinching. Some claim the Belgian government gave the order for their paratroopers to retreat from the Technical School in Kigali, so that the Hutus could get on with killing all the Tutsis who had sought refuge there. They say four thousand people died.'

'Four thousand Tutsis left to their deaths,' I say, 'to avoid ten paratroopers being killed. A Rwandan corpse will never be worth as much as a Belgian one.'

Emmanuelle gets up and I watch her elderly gait. Even though she's no older than me, she drags her feet like an old woman and dresses like one too: in long skirts. Could any of the Nyamirambo boys claim to have glimpsed Emmanuelle's thigh?

'Shall we pray?' she asks.

I want to shout: Pray! Pray! I've had enough of this Christian religion. I've lost my husband and I don't know where my children are, and you're asking me to pray? I hold myself back, more out of tact – I still need Emmanuelle – than out of respect for her faith. She's a Hutu, after all; she's not risking anything. No, that's not fair; Emmanuelle is risking her life hiding me. Why is grief making me so mean? I calm down.

'You know, Emmanuelle, a few weeks ago I saw some French soldiers in Kigali, all blacked up. They were going to support the Rwandan Armed Forces against the rebels. There were some real blacks among them. From the Antilles, no doubt.'

'Do you mean to say that France has betrayed us?'

'What I'm saying is that France is complicit in this genocide. Catholic France supports Sindikubwabo like it supported Habyarimana.'

I'm pleased with my treachery. Emmanuelle lowers her head, but then she suggests we pray for François Mitterrand. She's incorrigible.

We hear cries in the bush and bursts of automatic gunfire, another attack. I rush back into my hiding place under the sink, folding myself in awkwardly. Eventually, exhausted, I'm lulled to sleep by the crackling of gunfire in the distance.

# 13

O birds of my country!

Two resonant notes, shy in the waning dark. They sound out again, three, four, five times. In the distance, a response of two similar notes. Nearby, another bird joins in. Back and forth, four notes in conversation. Then a Heuglin's robin sounds his three somewhat plaintive tones, and another replies like an echo. An ibis enters the symphony with his strange strangled cry and soon all of Rwanda is vibrating with birdsong. It's like a gathering where everyone talks at the same time, but people still, somehow, understand each other. Birds are better than men at listening while talking: there's no shouting or anger in their songs.

I no longer welcome the birdsong because it prevents me from being able to hear my enemies approach. A dog barks in the distance, then a cockerel signals that it's time to get up. The genocidaires don't obey, though, they're still resting after the night's work.

The door to my hiding place opens suddenly, almost brutally. I have to close my eyes so as not to be dazzled by the light.

'All the Tutsis who have fallen will rise again. I declare it in Imana's name.'

I recognize my sister Hilde's voice. With difficulty, I open my eyes. Hilde has become an old wreck of a woman. But she smiles sweetly.

'We will all be saved. We will reign over Rwanda. We'll be respected by everyone.'

She stamps her feet on the spot in a nervous kind of dance.

'Hilde! Stop it, you'll get us noticed. They'll kill us.'

My words still her. She turns to face me; she has bulging eyes, sunken cheeks, a wild air. Hilde says all of Nyamirambo knows that I'm hiding here, and that's why she's come.

'I must tell you what God told me at night: that all the Tutsis will rise again immediately, so there's no need to fear the Hutus.'

'Do you have any news of my children?'

'Your children? They'll rise again. God told me so.'

'Did you see them die?'

'But they'll rise again.'

Hilde's words paralyze me. My mouth hangs open as heavy blows rain inside my temples. Tears want to come but don't. I'm shaking all over.

Emmanuelle appears and tries to calm Hilde down, but she has lost her mind.

'Madam, I'm going to the roadblock! I must announce that the Tutsis will rise again.'

Hilde shakes with nervous spasms, her eyes rove like a hunted beast. Then suddenly she calms down, smiles tenderly and looks up to the sky.

'Thank you, God, for having given the Tutsis immortality.'

Emmanuelle holds her firmly by the wrists.

'Hilde, Hilde, have you seen Yolande's children? Did you see them die? Tell us!'

'No, the Tutsis are not dead. They are immortal. God protects them.'

A door slams over at Déo's house. I shut the sink doors quickly. Déo shouts that there's a Tutsi in the vicinity, that she should give herself up. He walks in.

'But what are you doing here, Emmanuelle, with a Tutsi in your arms?'

'It's a woman who has gone mad. She came into the garden and started shouting. I'm trying to calm her down.'

'A Tutsi! I knew it. I'm taking her to the roadblock.'

Hilde interrupts kindly: 'Don't trouble yourself. I'm going there straight away to announce that Tutsis are the people chosen by God.'

They move away together and I can't hear any more.

So are my children dead? Or does Hilde no longer know what she's talking about? Emmanuelle returns a little later and tells me that I must stay hopeful and keep praying. I will live for another ten days like this. On the first day, I learn that my sister Hilde was executed at the roadblock. She smiled under the machete blow. Emmanuelle tells me that even dead, she was still smiling. I feel a little lump in my stomach, like a hernia. During the night, Emmanuelle lets me out of my hiding place. Outside, I make out a pile of sheet metal that used to form the roof of Spérancie's house, where my children were hiding. Déo has collected them. So where are my children?

On the second day, I learn that my cousin from Kibungo has been killed at the roadblock and three monks were killed in Gikongoro, amongst others. Something digs into my left breast. I find a biro in my shirt pocket. Aha! What if I wrote down the dates of the main events? But on what? And where are my children?

On the third day, I hear that my brother Nepo, the one who prophesied my survival, has been killed, but that evening I'm told it's not true, even though Emmanuelle saw a soldier driving my brother's minibus. That night I manage to pee a couple of drops. Where are my children?

On the fourth day, I learn that some friends from Cyangugu were executed at a roadblock. Meanwhile, Mayimuna, that blasted air hostess who wanted to cut off my breasts, has been seen in army uniform. I find an empty packet of cigarettes in the pocket of my jeans, unfold it carefully and write:

6 April: assassination of the President of the Republic.

13 April: Joseph is shot at the roadblock.

14 April: Joseph is finished off. My children are tortured.

15 April: My children disappear.

16 April: Hilde is killed.

My vocation as a writer ends there for now. But I know that one day I will write more. If I escape death, that is. Where are my children?

On the fifth day, I hear that my old professor from Ruhengeri has been executed. The same day, Mzee, a boy who works for Emmanuelle, places his cooker in front of my door. I realize he knows that Emmanuelle is hiding a Tutsi in here. Still, I'm sure he'll protect me, because his mistress is protecting me, as if the bonds of servitude are stronger than blood. My little lump has disappeared. Where are my children?

On the sixth day, I learn that my cousins from Byumba have been executed at a roadblock. The wife was like a madwoman. 'I'm not a Tutsi, I'm a Hutu,' she said in tears to the militia man examining her identity card.

'So why does it say that you're Tutsi then?'

'It's a mistake. I'm a Hutu.'

A machete blow ended the discussion.

Also, Boutros Boutros-Ghali has apologized in front of the UN for not having grasped the seriousness of the Rwandan crisis. Out of my hiding place briefly, I look at myself in a mirror. Tatters of skin hang down my cheeks like a dog's ears. Where are my children?

On the seventh day, I hear that a friend from Kibuye was executed at a roadblock. Christians have asked the Cardinal, whose name I can't remember, to say a mass in memory of the victims of the Rwandan massacres. I've completely stopped urinating. Well, it's more practical this way. Where are my children?

On the eighth day, I learn that ten young people were killed in Gitarama as they fled to Burundi. That night, I weigh myself on Emmanuelle's scales: thirty-seven kilos. I laugh. Where are my children?

On the ninth day, I hear that the RPF forces have begun attacking Nyamirambo hill. A little bit later, the news is denied, then reconfirmed, then denied again. I lose my sight for three hours and then I can see again. Where are my children?

In these nine days, I get to know my benefactor, Emmanuelle. I'm still not sure whether I hate or love her, but I both admire and despise her. I check her head for lice. I don't like the way she drags her feet, her air of a sweet Madonna and her daily calls for prayer. I don't like her long dresses that hide everything.

Every night, we speak for several hours by candlelight. Emmanuelle makes me instant soup that she presents to me dutifully, but I can only take two or three spoonfuls. I spend hours looking at her little face, as thin as an anorexic's, planted on top of her plump little body. Her eyes dart around as though trying to avoid mine and she scratches her lips as she speaks in such an irritating way.

One night, I ask her why she never got married.

'There is only one man I love,' she bursts out. 'He lives in Burundi. And he's married.'

From her tone, I know not to ask her about it again. But she brings it up again on another evening.

'You know, my legs are too fat for me to get married.'

I look at her legs. All I can see is a long grey skirt, and at the bottom ten toes, scrunched up against the ground like a child protecting herself from an imminent blow.

One night, she asks me, 'Would you recognize a T-shirt with "Indianapolis" written on it?'

'Yes. It's Sandrine's. An American friend gave it to me.'

'That's what I thought. I've seen one of Déo's children wearing it.'

She looks at the bottom of her teacup. I imagine Immaculée, Déo's daughter who I treated for rheumatic fever, wearing the T-shirt.

'You don't mean to say that...' Words escape me.

Emmanuelle looks at me sadly. It's the first time in days that she's looked me in the eyes. I don't want to understand the message. No. My children are not dead. She doesn't know anything. It's impossible. I make myself smile. I've still got hope. You can find 'Indianapolis' T-shirts anywhere.

I feel a gush of love for Emmanuelle. There's no need to resent her for not being under a death threat. She's endangering herself by hiding me. But is it out of love for me or love for Christ? Because Christian love is unconditional, it sometimes seems inhuman. I feel like a chicken being protected from the knife by a fanatical vegetarian. There is no common ground between someone who has faith and someone who has lost it. I admire Emmanuelle's courage, risking her life to save mine, but I despise her religious motives.

My feelings trouble me. Is it hunger that is making my head spin? I begin to feel a kind of love for the genocidaires. Or is it pity? Am I losing my mind like Hilde? I feel drawn to them. I tell myself I should go to the roadblock and give myself up. Delirious, I think that they're right to want to kill me because I'm a cowardly woman. That I've just understood the point of the genocide and I'll bend joyfully to the new law. That I no longer deserve to live: I must pay for ancient mistakes. That the Interahamwe are right to want to clean up the country. That Rwanda is their country, not mine. That if they love me a little they must kill me.

I see André's machete in the bush again. I long for it to cut my neck. 'If you love me, kill me!' I cry. It seems to me I must atone for being a Tutsi, an unforgivable fault.

I have one more enemy: myself.

# 14

I t begins on the morning of the tenth day. First, loud muffled bangs, two at a time: one from the send-off, one from the explosion. Missiles launched with explosives, sophisticated weapons that frighten you twice. And then the whole hill becomes a battlefield.

Emmanuelle is beside herself. 'It's raining bombs,' she says, through the door. 'Everyone is running everywhere and they're searching houses again.'

She opens my door: 'You've got to go, before Déo comes back and finds you!' I don't move. 'Don't you realize the RPF forces are attacking us? People are running mad! Some want to flee, others want to finish off the remaining Tutsis before they leave. It's a mess.'

'But if the rebels arrive, I'll be free.'

'You'll be dead before they arrive. They're talking about burning down all the houses before they take off.'

Emmanuelle pulls me out of my hiding place. 'Go! Run!'

'But where?'

'I don't know!'

Once again I play my trump card and crawl towards Déo's kitchen. Just outside, I find myself face to face with Pauline. She looks at me warily and orders me to leave.

I laugh in her face. 'I know you're hiding other Tutsis, so one more, what difference does it make?'

She recoils. I enter her kitchen by force.

'Déo's going to arrive any moment now,' says Pauline fearfully.

I slide into the help's bedroom, next to the kitchen. I know Mzee won't betray me. Mzee who put his cooker in front of my hiding place to dissuade the Interahamwe from searching under the sink. I slide under his bed and bump into someone else, who moves over to give me a little more space. My feet stick out, so I get out, find a basin we can use, slide back under the bed, and with my toes manage to pull the basin over our four feet. I hear Déo's voice, full of pride:

'I'm sure I know where Muganga is.'

He comes into Mzee's bedroom like a gust of wind. He sounds agitated.

Pauline calls him back to the kitchen: 'Come Déo, come. Stop looking for cockroaches. You've done your duty. You've killed one with your own hands. Nobody is asking you to be more zealous.'

'I want to finish my work...'

Under the bed, I begin to understand that killing is like making love. The first time it frightens you. Afterwards you acquire a taste for it.

Emmanuelle appears and Déo throws a torrent of abuse at her, shouting that she's only got a few more minutes to live because now everyone knows that she's hiding Muganga under her sink. 'Now you're afraid, aren't you?'

'I'm not afraid.' I imagine Emmanuelle smiling.

'You're dying of fear! I can see it.'

'Let's go together and look under my sink. But first, let's make a pact. If you find Muganga there you have the right to kill me. If you don't find her, you must apologize.'

'Me, apologize, have you gone mad or something?'

I hear Déo dragging Emmanuelle away. After a few moments, he yells out in anger at finding nothing. He's been tricked, someone had sworn that Muganga was under this sink, someone lied to him. A shower of missiles interrupts him, and they return to take refuge in the kitchen. A huge explosion: a shell must have landed right here in the garden. From the sound of things, on top of the stolen sheets of metal. The attack lasts around fifteen minutes, stopping life on the hill.

After three minutes of silence, Déo announces that he's going to the roadblock to tell them that Muganga must have hidden somewhere else.

I turn to the person sharing my hiding place and finally recognize my cousin, Solange! We laugh at the coincidence and then hug in tears. I don't want to put her in even more danger, so I slide out, and crawl back to my sink. I get in as best I can, but after two minutes I can't take it any longer, I get out again.

No, I can't hide myself indefinitely. I want to give myself up at the roadblock so that everything will be over. I actually want them to execute me with one sharp blow but I'm afraid of being raped. Perhaps it's the fear of being raped that gives me strength. I move to Emmanuelle's kitchen, a long badly lit room, and find Solange there, drinking some water at the table. We look at each other for a long time, silently; an intimate conversation between women who can read each other's eyes. Then we talk and agree that if one of us is taken, she won't reveal where the other is hiding. We swear, we hug.

Déo's voice. I have just enough time to throw myself behind the door. Thanks be to Imana who protects the Tutsi! The door moves on its hinges. I try without success to make it cover me again.

Déo notices Solange. 'Please leave my house. Go! Give yourself up at the roadblock. Everything is over now for the Tutsis. I don't want to have any trouble.'

'I won't go to the roadblock, Déo.'

'Then at least go and hide yourself in John's house with the other Tutsis.'

The bastards! They're gathering up the Tutsis, before deciding what to do with them.

Déo is almost opposite me, but somehow, doesn't see me. Solange gets up and moves around the table as she talks so that Déo will turn his back to me. Then she gets on the offensive:

'If you're a man, kill me right here. You know how to use your machete, go ahead, cut off my head. Eh! But you don't have it in you from what I can see. You don't know how to kill.'

What courage! Déo edges backwards, almost afraid.

'I know how to kill snakes,' he says, 'but there's only one snake that interests me. It's Muganga. I'll leave the others to the beginners.'

His voice trembles; he doesn't have the guts to perform a second execution. He leaves, shouting back at Solange that he'll order the neighbourhood children to search the whole area until they find Muganga.

I can't believe Déo found himself face to face with me and didn't see me. Solange gets up, comes towards me, hugs me. 'I'm going. I'll look for somewhere else to hide. Stay strong.'

I agree, but for the first time since the assassination of Habyarimana, I feel truly afraid. Where are my children?

I have no choice but to hide under the sink once more. Emmanuelle returns a little later, and puts her cooker down in front of my door.

'In the whole neighbourhood there are only four Tutsi women left. They've just executed the last seven men.'

'And my children?'

'I don't know, Yolande. I don't know where they are.'

'And Spérancie?'

'I don't know.'

'And Sophie, my friend Sophie?'

'I don't know. She disappeared at the beginning. Nobody knows where she is. Some say she made it to Burundi.'

'And Rukara, who did our ironing?'

'I think he was one of the seven who were executed just now.'

'Listen, Emmanuelle, this can't go on. Either I go to the roadblock to end it all or I must leave the neighbourhood. If I go to the roadblock, I'll be raped, they'll cut off my breasts and I don't know what else, so I'm going to try to leave the neighbourhood. At least, if they catch me at a roadblock where I'm not known, they won't feel the need to rape me, killing me will be enough. Listen carefully: I've left several hundred dollars with the parish priests. Get the money, then go to Kigali and look for a soldier you can bribe to get me out of here. Tell him I'm a Hutu married to a Tutsi. We can flee together. There's no doubt Déo wants to kill you too: he's convinced you're hiding Tutsis.'

Emmanuelle refuses. 'It's better to pray,' she says. 'Put yourself in God's hands.'

'Imana? He got us into this mess in the first place!'

'Not Imana, our Saviour Jesus Christ.'

'Your Saviour Jesus-whatever has abandoned us well and good, wouldn't you say?'

'He never abandons anyone, Yolande. That's blasphemy!'

This talk infuriates me. 'I'm sorry, you're right. But I saw the Saviour in a dream last night. He asked me to leave the neighbourhood by any means possible.'

'The Saviour appeared to you in a dream?'

'Yes, Emmanuelle. I didn't dare tell you.'

'Well then, I'll do everything you ask me to. But you know I can't walk. My feet are in pain.'

'The Saviour told me they would heal as you walked.'

Emmanuelle is overcome, ready for anything, almost smiling. She leaves right away.

'I'll be back this evening.'

The shells keep raining down until dusk. Then the wait for Emmanuelle begins. Someone must have been taken nearby because I hear cries, whistles. Killing must be thirsty work: soon afterwards I hear a noise like a large coconut being opened, with a club no doubt. Indifferent, the crickets begin. But what is Emmanuelle doing? Where is she? What if it was her they just executed?

The isolation, discomfort and hunger send me into a metaphysical spin. Why was I born? I answer myself: everyone is born, everyone could ask why and that wouldn't get us anywhere. But my tired mind doesn't give up. Why did I have a happy childhood? Why did I love my parents? Did they need my love, they who loved each other like Romeo and Juliet? Why did I study, get married, have children? The spiral of life frightens me. Where are my children? Why have children in a country torn apart by hate? Why live? I feel useless, stupid, like

I'm too much. Why was I so afraid of being a widow? Why was I so afraid to see my children cry? My absurd questions boil down to the same one: Why am I suffering so much? Suffering with a pain buried deep inside my body.

I know that I'll never be able to adequately express what I live through under my sink. I know that suffering is inexpressible when the cause of it is irreversible.

Where are my children? Have I reached the point yet where I wish they'd never been born?

# 15

**E**mmanuelle is right in front of me, in tears.

'I've never seen such horror.'

'Did you succeed?'

'There were bodies everywhere.'

'Did you get my money from the priests?'

'They've made roadblocks with corpses. There's an unbearable smell throughout Kigali.'

'What did the priests say?'

'I walked along the tarmacked road for two kilometres and saw nothing but corpses.'

'Do you have my money?'

'I saw a woman dying in agony, with a headwound, moaning, begging for someone to finish her off.'

'But Emmanuelle, tell me, were you able to get my money from the priests?'

'They have dug pits and bulldozers are pushing the bodies in, all jumbled up. I even saw a dog making off with an arm in its mouth.'

I can't get anything out of her in this state of shock, so I let her speak. She tells me about the thousands of horrors she saw on the road. She seems to take pleasure in describing the corpses, she needs to talk about the corpses.

Do I need to imagine the dead bodies? Joseph's corpse was enough for me.

I hear a kind interior music: women humming a tune I've never heard before. I see passing before my eyes corpses that I've never seen, as if I myself am moving, retracing

Emmanuelle's long road to Calvary, seeing what she describes. I see roads strewn with men, their skulls smashed in. I see a five-year-old child hanging from the branch of a cedar tree, one foot still wearing a shoe. I see the roadblock of burning tyres. I see a woman writhing in pain on the bare ground. I see two Interahamwe laying into the dead with machetes, as if to prove a point: they hate them even if they didn't have enough courage to kill them themselves. I see houses in flames, the bush in flames, men in flames running in every direction. I see the MINUAR jeeps driving around the corpses. I see queues of Tutsis waiting to be tortured. I see a man whose feet have been cut off crawling along the tarmac. I see half-filled graves of corpses, some, against all logic, still calling for help. I see detached arms and legs, left for the dogs. I see Kigali, one evening during the genocide. I see it without seeing it, as described by Emmanuelle. And I hear again, RTLM calling for genocide ten days ago.

Where is my Rwanda? Where are my children?

Emmanuelle takes me out of my nightmare. She tells me that at one roadblock, they tried to claim that her Hutu identity card was a forgery. She only managed to escape death by pretending she too hated snakes. Elsewhere, they asked why she was travelling despite the curfew. To save her Hutu father-in-law who had been taken hostage by the Tutsis, she claimed. Entering central Kigali, an officer felt her up while searching her. She prayed not to be raped and God heard her.

Emmanuelle continues on, half demented, until I have an idea:

'Shall we pray?'

We pray for a long time, while shells continue to fall, and I get bored. But the prayers work; Emmanuelle comes back to earth. Yes, she got the dollars from the priest with a strange name... Father Vanoverschelden, that's right. Yes, she managed to reach Kigali, where she found a soldier who would rescue me, but only if I were a Hutu.

'And what did you say?'

'That you're a Hutu, even though your mother was a Tutsi. But there's worse. He asked me for the money straight away.'

'You gave him my money?'

'I had to, he demanded it. That's why I'm afraid he won't return.'

'You must be mad!'

'He gave me his word that he'd come to get you.'

'What worth is the word of a soldier corrupted by this regime?'

'He's a Hutu, but from the South. I'm sure he'll come.'

I fall into a daze, I can't listen to any more. I ask Emmanuelle if she's seen people drinking coconut milk?

'Coconut milk? No. Not at all.'

'I thought I heard the Interahamwe breaking coconuts.'

'You must have been dreaming.'

'But why are the Hutus of the South…?'

I don't finish my question. I know the answer, but I ask as if I no longer believed it. Emmanuelle explains patiently that the Hutus from the South are afraid of the Hutus from the North; that the genocide won't spare southerners because they're not from Habyarimana's region.

I look at her, still in a daze. I know, but I don't know all that. Have I forgotten the North-South divide in Rwandan politics? Genocide has made me go mad like my sister Hilde. I might as well go to the roadblock, so that I no longer have to live with this awareness of genocide.

'I'm going to the roadblock. I'm guilty of being a Tutsi. I can't bear it anymore! I shout, moan, cry. I've lost all self-control.

All of a sudden, I'm hit by a wave of cold water. Emmanuelle has thrown a bucket of water at my face: it runs down, soaking my shirt. I come back to myself again. What happened?

'Nothing, Yolande. You just lost your head for a moment. Don't worry, a soldier is coming tonight to take you to a safe place.'

'A soldier? What soldier?'

'The one you asked me to bribe.'

'I asked you to lead a soldier astray?'

Emmanuelle pushes me back under my sink like a sardine into a box, gets a pair of scissors and cuts my long hair haphazardly.

'You mustn't be recognized.'

I'm too weak to resist or even protest. In less time than it takes to tell, I'm shaved like a sinner. Emmanuelle slides the door closed and I just let everything happen: I have no strength left. I feel like a jack-in-the-box with a broken spring. I won't have the energy to surprise the militia man who comes to kill me. I'm a dead woman. I don't even have the strength to ask about my children.

My children? At times, I imagine them dead, laid out on the tarmac: a passing militia man gives them a useless kick, to prove that he knows how to hate. At other times, I see them still hiding in the banana plantation, at the foot of the hill in Nyamirambo. They're there, all three of them, taking turns to look out for enemies. They're hungry, they're thin, but they're alive. I see Christian picking a banana or digging up a potato and giving it to his sisters. I hear Sandrine comforting Nadine and I feel Nadine pressing herself against me. I dream, alone, under my sink.

It takes less effort to settle myself now I've become so thin. My buttocks have completely disappeared, and I can slip my hips under the U-bend that hovers like a question mark above my belly button. How much have I changed? I want to see myself. A ray of light brushes my jeans as I undress with fastidious contortions. I look at the hollow of my stomach. Three points emerge: two bones sticking out of my pelvis and my prominent pubic bone, covered in black hair. It looks like the Virunga volcanoes. I live for a moment in this reclaimed intimacy. Although I've lost flesh, I'm still a woman. Hope washes over me once more. I pass my hand over my bare scalp and feel the unexpected bumps of my skull. No, I haven't yet lost all hope.

# 16

**R**wanda no longer matters to me. I'm abandoning my sweet hill in Nyamirambo. I have no country.

The soldier pulls open my door roughly. It is dark and I'm cold, but I'm not afraid, even though my meagre sanctuary has been breached. His angular face stands out against the twilight sky. His eyes gleam. He turns to Emmanuelle and exclaims:

'What an old woman! You told me she was still young. You misled me.'

'She's still young; she's not even forty.'

'She looks sixty, at least. And what's more, she's a Tutsi. I'm sure of it. I should kill her, but I'll save her because I keep my word. An old woman like her won't have any more Tutsi children. Get yourselves ready. You've four minutes to make it to the bottom of the path where I've hidden the van.'

The man shuts my door as brutally as he opened it.

Darkness.

I'm not afraid. But I am cold. I'm getting colder and colder…

Emmanuelle opens up at last, sets me free. But my legs fail to work.

'Be brave, Yolande. Your life depends on it.'

'And my children, where are my children?'

'Don't think about your children right now. Nobody knows where they are, maybe even they don't know. Get up.'

'Get up and walk!' I say, laughing weakly. 'It's so easy to say. You're not Christ, you know!'

Somehow, I manage to stand on my two legs. They are like two stems, as fragile as reeds, and I sway on top of them, trembling.

'I'm at the end of my strength, Emmanuelle. I can't take another step. Just leave me to die here.'

'After everything I've done for you? After all my pleas to God? No! You'll get up and you'll walk around the garden, and you'll get into the soldier's vehicle.'

'I'm finished.'

'You'll do it! No more discussions.'

Emmanuelle's authoritative tone fills me with pride: she believes in my strength. Very well, I'll be strong.

'You're right, I'm off. And you?'

'I'll join you on the road, as if nothing unusual is going on. It's safer, because Déo is watching my comings and goings. Go.'

Go? It's the first time since the death of Habyarimana that I obey an order. It's perhaps the first time in my life! I'm an independent woman by nature, but tonight I am beaten. Tonight, I'm a slave of this country: of a Rwanda that kills and a Rwanda that protects.

A new energy fills me. I edge my way between the fences, slide over a gate like a snake, and come face to face with a child tied to a tree. It's Joker, a local child who has always had trouble learning. His mother was killed six days ago. Whenever he sees anyone he lets out a surprised grunt, 'Memmm...' which used to make my children laugh and his mother cry. Joker is tied to a tree. He is starved, his trousers have slid down to his knees, showing his underwear, stained with excrement. His head has fallen onto his shoulder, only his eyes are still moving. They follow me, watch me, trust me. I pray that he won't let out his usual lowing greeting because that will give me away. I crawl to his feet. If only I had a knife. I think of the Claude François song, 'Si j'avais un marteau, If I had a hammer...' It's stupid, it's what comes to mind. If I had a knife I'd set this child free. But what for after all? I feel like I'm losing my mind again. What if I gave myself up at the roadblock? Why not let everything go? If Joker cries out I'll be captured and saved from this nightmare by death. Would a machete blow to the nape of my neck hurt that much? Wouldn't it be a quick death? If my children are dead, what's the point of carrying on? But what if they're alive?

Two men pass, and I huddle under a hibiscus hedge for a moment. A small grass snake slides between two roots. It seems even more afraid than I am. Afraid? Yes, my fear has returned. It had disappeared with the hope of escape, but they have returned together. My fear shows me I'm still hopeful, so I continue to crawl forward until my head hits a car tyre.

'Finally, you're here!'

The soldier lifts me up by my armpits, and sends me hurtling head-first into the passenger cab of his pickup truck, behind the three seats that he pulls down immediately, not caring if he breaks my ribs. A conspiratorial silence reigns, broken only by the sound of two doors shutting and the purring of the motor. The vehicle bounces along the uneven path, and with every rut a metallic bar digs into my stomach. A stop.

'Papers!'

'Army Lieutenant!'

'Tutsis?'

'No snakes with us. I'm doing the rounds. Do you have all the arms you need?'

'We're short on ammunition, Lieutenant. We're obliged to work with machetes.'

'Noted. See you soon.'

'See you soon, Lieutenant!'

The van sets off again. Another stop, the same exchange. I can hear from his voice that this soldier is even more afraid than I am. We stop and go through five or six roadblocks over less than a kilometre. At one, a beam of light makes me shiver as it lingers over the vehicle's seats, and fixes itself for a long while on the faces of Emmanuelle and the soldier.

'Look carefully at this photograph,' says a voice. 'Do you know this person?'

'Never seen her.'

'Do you know who it is?'

'Yes. It's Muganga Yolande, but I don't know how I know.'

'Good. And you say you've never seen her?'

'Yes, now I remember! I saw her three or four weeks ago; I took an injured soldier to her clinic.'

'Ah! So you know her then?'

'I only saw her once.'

'You! Where were you born?'

'In Butare.'

'So you're an army man from the South?'

'No! My parents are from Gisenyi.'

Gisenyi, that magical word! President Habyarimana's homeland. Just say 'Gisenyi' and you'll be safe. They let us pass. I'll never know whether the soldier recognized me in the photo they showed to him.

We reach the Nyamirambo parish church. Just yesterday morning, right here, hundreds of fleeing people were killed by soldiers apparently not au fait with the notion of asylum. A roadblock has been set up opposite the priests' house so we can't stop there, and instead drive to the back of the church. The soldier pulls me out like a sack of potatoes and throws me into a bush. I feel a thousand prickles; it's an acacia.

'When the truck's out of earshot, count to a hundred... then do as you please.' He is still extremely nervous.

'Be brave, Yolande,' Emmanuelle says. I hear her parting words but from my thorn bush can barely make out her face through the windows, and I know she can't see me. The soldier keeps his lights off as the truck disappears, but turns them on further down the road. The soldier turns from treason to genocide once more. But on the balance sheet of Tutsis he's killed we can add one soul that he's saved, albeit for money! Hundreds of dollars to find myself one kilometre further away, what a high price! But I've just received the most beautiful present: I've just understood that a genocidaire isn't always a monster. I've just understood that evil always comes from weakness. And sometimes goodness does too.

I count to a hundred, cheating like a child playing hide and seek, then crawl towards the priests' house next to the church. I must cross about forty metres in the open, and can see the roadblock nearby where the Interahamwe are talking. When one of them gets up, I stop still. The street lights are too feeble to expose me, but I'm afraid a militia man might do a turn around the priests' garden. I'm afraid? Then I'm alive! The priests' door is sheltered from sight. I'm just about to ring when it opens.

Someone says: 'I've been watching you for the last ten minutes. Emmanuelle called me this afternoon to let me know you were coming. Come in, Yolande.'

'Father Vanoverschelden? Father Vanoverschelden?'

I begin to cry. Ah, my tears have returned! I can cry again! Even if I only have a couple of tears left.

'Father Vanoverschelden!'

I make an idiotic gesture: I press myself against him. I'd like him to hold me in his arms, to open them wide like the arms of Christ.

I repeat his name. He says nothing, so I apologize. He tells me that there's nothing to apologize for.

'Father Vanoverschelden, you're so good!'

I sense that I've just lied.

# 17

enter a large room set aside for people seeking shelter. The priests have taken out all of the furniture and a streetlamp outside casts a bluish light through the bars of the high windows onto a white wall. The ground is strewn with bodies, half-asleep. Children gesturing as they moan, fat and flabby women, their baggy skin spread out. One is feeding a newborn, her enormous breast on display. Another is curled up around a little boy snoring gently; he is half naked, and his head is covered with a white bandage. A wrinkled old woman leans against the wall, her breathing barely perceptible, a sleeping child between her legs.

Those awake turn to look at me, then drop their eyes. Two women seem to signal to each other, saying what, I don't know, but I can tell they don't want me to understand them. I hear someone murmuring the word I've hated since 6 April: Muganga. This word, that people used to honour me, that I was proud of, now rings out like a death sentence. Muganga! While once it meant doctor, today it means riches, jealousy, possible gains for informants. And yet I know nearly all these women. I've treated three quarters of them, helped at least ten here give birth. They're nearly all Hutu farmers, with a few Tutsi women gathered in a corner.

I sense their fear; everyone knows that Muganga is the most wanted person in Nyamirambo. I'm a target and my presence makes even the most innocent of Hutus feel afraid. The Hutu women here made the mistake of marrying Tutsi men, and their husbands are dead. The Interahamwe would also like to relieve Rwanda of their children; 'Hutsi,' they're called in contempt. And if they learn that Muganga is hiding here, there would be even less pity for these children. And yet I'm in the same situation as they are. I'm no longer Muganga. I'm nothing more than a fleeing woman, like thousands of other Rwandans.

I don't want to flee. I'm a mother. I don't want to believe my children are dead. Nobody has actually seen them die. There is not one witness. When I ask questions I always receive evasive replies: 'We haven't seen them in a while; it would make sense that they've been killed. They've disappeared.'

Father Vanoverschelden doesn't know anything either, nor does Father Tadeuz, a Czech who speaks Kinyarwanda with a funny accent.

'Father Tadeuz, where are your Belgian colleagues?'

'Returned to Brussels. Evacuated by the UN. Go to bed.'

His reply is laconic and closes down any further questions.

Even the bathroom has been transformed into a dormitory. It hardly matters, since there's no more running water. The priests have reserved the room for Tutsi adolescent girls and named it Mu Bwiza, meaning 'The Beautiful Ones', after a district in Bujumbura.

'If the Interahamwe come to search the house, hopefully they won't check the bathroom and the girls won't be raped.'

I glance in. Fifteen sets of teeth smile at me. A girl gets up and comes to hug me.

'I love you, Muganga. I'll pray for you.'

'What is your name?'

'Béata. You cured my malaria last year. I didn't have any money and you said I could pay later.'

'Thank you, Béata, you've just paid me.'

I still have friends in Rwanda.

Father Tadeuz shows me a room set aside for old women.

'You're not old just yet,' he says, laughing, 'but if you could see yourself you'd understand why I'm putting you in this room. In any case, you'll be safer among those whom nobody wants to rape.' His eyes twinkle with mischief.

This reminds me that I have my period.

'Father Tadeuz, it's my time of the month. What can I do?'

'Wait here. Father Vanoverschelden will come back in just a minute.'

I greet the old women. 'Good evening!'

No one responds. Reluctantly, one of the women moves back a little to give me some space to sit down. My heart jolts in fear, thinking I recognize the mother of Alphonse, a Hutu extremist who laments, or so I'm told, not having been able to murder his Tutsi fiancée who is travelling in Europe. What is she doing here? Is she spying on us? I look at the old woman surreptitiously. She raises her head slowly. No, it can't be her! Her eyes are filled with tears. She murmurs weakly:

'I am a Tutsi, Yolande.'

Now I understand. She is indeed Alphonse's mother, but despite everything her son wants to find and kill her.

Father Vanoverschelden comes back ten minutes later with a pair of yellow pyjamas, a large pair of men's underwear, open at the front, and a handful of sanitary pads, almost spotless, recovered from the corpses in the church.

'Go wash yourself.'

He gives me a milk-powder tin filled with water. This will be my ration.

'Don't make any noise; you might be heard from the roadblock.'

Father Vanoverschelden's tone is firm, almost cold. Is he afraid too?

'My father, I would like to ask if –'

'Silence. We'll talk about it tomorrow. Go wash and then lie down. It's an order, Yolande.'

A shower! These buildings have only one shower, and it's dry now. The priests go out regularly to look for water, under the mocking eye of the Interahamwe, who know that they're hiding women and children. The militia don't care; they know they'll catch any Tutsis amongst us sooner or later. I'm told they visit regularly to count everyone and sometimes take people away, most often children they drag screaming from their mothers' arms. They look for Muganga, and are enraged not to find her.

Father Vanoverschelden gives me an identity card he found on a corpse. I'm now called Nyiramana Xaverina. I carry the name of a dead woman. Perhaps I'm dead and I don't even know it. I feel like a zombie: one of those souls of the dead that, according to Caribbean pagan traditions, are woken up by sorcerers to do their bidding. With my shaved head and air of a sixty-year-old woman, I doubt the Interahamwe will recognize me. In a mirror the size of a packet of cigarettes, I discover some white hair.

I pour a little water into the palms of my hands carefully and let it trickle over my body. The feel of it tracing a path across my skin reminds me of Joseph. The water washes off bits of plants and lumps of earth that had been squeezed between my buttocks. I watch them jostling to go down the plughole. They disintegrate, giving the water a reddish ochre tint. A cockroach struggles before drowning; was he lodged in the remaining tufts of my hair or between my thighs? I ask him if he too feels like a victim of the genocide.

'You're a cockroach; you must die like all the Tutsi!'

I relish my own cruelty for a moment. In response, the cockroach disappears down the plughole, drowned. I laugh at my stupidity. Muganga who talks to the insects!

Outside, I hear shots, cries, whistles. The usual.

Father Vanoverschelden bursts in.

'Quick, quick. You must hide.'

'But I'm naked!'

'So what?'

Vanoverschelden pushes me into a bedroom that has an open Bible on a rattan prayer stand. It must be the room of one of the priests who fled to Europe.

'Don't sleep in the bed, it's too dangerous.'

'Yes, my Father. Goodnight.'

'Goodnight, Yolande.'

The door closes and I get into the bed. To me, it's like one of those luxurious four-poster beds you see in the movies, where you imagine the nights are soft. In fact, it's a terrible kapok mattress thrown onto a sprung bedstead. But I haven't lain in a bed for fifteen days. The white man has a certain smell; I inhale it, I try to work out the different notes. The fact that I'm sleeping in the bed of a white priest amuses me. Between the shells and the whistles, I pass the most beautiful night of my life.

# 18

L ike a silent bell, Father Vanoverschelden moves from room to room inviting people to come to mass. He knocks gently, opens the door halfway, joins his hands together with the air of a mischievous actor, and goes on his way, leaving the door ajar.

Mass. An empty dining room, the tables pushed up against the walls, the faded pastel-coloured curtains closed. On one side, a tapestry cheers up the place with its bright colours; it must have been woven by the parishioners – there are recognizable banana trees, cows with graceful horns and in the distance several volcanoes. A wooden table serves as an altar, hurriedly covered with a nasty little tablecloth. Two wooden chalices await the celebrants. Thirty women sit on the floor, surrounded by their restless but silent children. Everyone knows to be quiet, even the newborns. There's a profound sadness in the air. Calloused hands distractedly finger red cedar rosaries, suspended above knees grey with dust. Each person murmurs her prayers automatically, under her breath, without looking around. A woman moans that her child has just peed on her cloth. She gets up, shakes it out, brings it to her nose, then sits down again. Mass can start.

I don't see the priests approach, nor do I hear their good words. Everything happens so fast, I don't even get up for the offertory.

I have a moment of fervour, though, for Emmanuelle, but it's atheist fervour. I pray to the goddess of fate, who comes straight out of my imagination, asking her to protect

Emmanuelle, who risked her life to save mine. I think of Côme and Déo, of those who cut off my husband's hand. No, I don't find any hatred in me; I'd only like them to see the harm they've done me. And when Father Vanoverschelden presents to the faithful the large wooden cross with Christ sculpted in low relief, by a Twa no doubt, I revolt at the idea that this man died to save all men. Christ couldn't save my husband Joseph! And where did he hide my children?

Usually, on religious holidays, Holy Communion is an occasion for truly Rwandan disorder, with people pushing each other as if they're at a football match. But today, it's a slow silent procession, like at a funeral when you're paying respects to the body in the coffin for the last time. One woman doesn't have the strength to get up and join the line so Father Vanoverschelden has to wind his way between the stretched-out legs to take the sacred host to her. At the end, he glances at me strangely; I'm the only one who hasn't taken communion.

Throughout the mass, a Hutsi child called Cadjos laughs and skips around. He doesn't know what death is; how could he know about murder? He is only five years old. An unbearable age. I love this child because he is innocent. He runs between the women, jumping over their slumped bodies, enchanted by all the frivolities of existence. No, I don't love Cadjos, I envy him. I hate him for not understanding the genocide. There's no genocide according to Cadjos. I love him again.

Father Vanoverschelden comes towards us with a piece of paper. I'm afraid that it's a list of the dead we should pray for. Silently, I beg him not to make us read this list. It will destroy our morale.

I can breathe again. It's only a prayer, asking God to forgive our killers. For a moment, I feel myself becoming Christian again. A fortnight of flight turned me into a pagan, but the kind that admires those who sacrifice themselves for others. Joseph had the strength to let himself be killed without revealing where I was hidden, why can't I find the strength to forgive those who want me dead? Just yesterday I was longing for the end, to give myself up at a roadblock. But thanks to these priests I have faith in life again. It's not a very Catholic faith but it keeps me going. Once more I want to live, live not for me but to bear witness. One day I will write a book, if I can. I will speak in the name of the Tutsi people. I will have pride once more.

My mind wanders further as the blessings continue. I have no idea whether I'm Christian or pagan, Tutsi or Hutu, Rwandan or European. I want to love the whole world and hate it at the same time. I want to shout out my distress and proclaim my love for my neighbours. I want to believe that everything is over and that everything will start again. I have gone mad. Where are my children?

We're interrupted by three loud knocks. Women scatter in every direction, but I remain calm, sitting, alone in front of the altar of fortune. I think neither of Christ, nor of Joseph, nor of my children; I think only of the genocide.

A woman climbs onto a table pushed against the windows and peers out at the Saint André secondary school.

'What are you looking at?'

'They've come looking for me. I'm sure of it. I want to say goodbye to Silas.'

'Silas, who's he?'

'My husband. He sought refuge at the school. Tomorrow is our wedding anniversary. I would so like to say goodbye.'

I climb onto the table in turn. You can just make out one of the school buildings. What are the chances that her husband is at a window at this very moment, waiting to wave at her? He's not.

'Now everything is over. You're called Yolande, aren't you? Do me this last favour, Yolande. When I am dead, let my husband know. That's all I ask. Let him know that I love him beyond death. My name is Eugénie.'

'I promise.'

We learn that it wasn't soldiers who knocked but new arrivals. Eugénie wants to keep talking. 'A few days ago, two MINUAR soldiers came and took a couple whose daughter is in Belgium, to drive them to Kanombe airport, where an airplane was waiting to take them to Brussels.'

I'm irritated, almost jealous. 'Why are you telling me this?'

'I'm telling you because it's the truth.'

Her response irritates me even more. Now I understand why whites get exasperated by how Rwandans talk; we don't respond to a question directly. We dance around it first with tangential considerations. I was trained by white teachers: maybe I'm too westernized to appreciate our ways.

'Why are you telling me this story about people protected by MINUAR?'

Eugénie smiles disarmingly: 'Because it's the truth, Yolande.'

Then she starts on an endless story about her own escape, how her husband hid in a false ceiling, how they duped the Interahamwe, how they got here. I think she's finally finished, but no, there's a second chapter. This one is about the daughter of the couple who were evacuated. She managed to get to Goma in the most fantastic way, took an airplane to Kinshasa, then on to Brussels, where she got in touch with the family of a Sergeant in MINUAR, and so on.

I begin to hate stories of flight, I even hate myself. But still she goes on: a third chapter! A MINUAR soldier from Togo came to the church with orders to evacuate the couple in question, but not the niece of the husband, who is also here. Eugénie describes a pathetic scene of heartbreak, but I can't listen any more. 'Where are my children?' I want to shout.

'You see, there's no solidarity amongst us,' she concludes sanctimoniously. 'That's why I'm telling you this story.'

As if I didn't know that! I realized it at the beginning of this conversation! I feel no more solidarity with everyone here than I do with people I don't know. Genocide has made strangers of us, even though we're united in our suffering.

I probably knew as much even yesterday. It's each person for him or herself. I begin to hate the Tutsi blood that flows through my veins. A little further away, Cadjos begins to sing. I want to strangle him.

# 19

I n Rwanda names aren't given like those in Europe.

My name is Mukagasana, which means 'the wife of Gasana', because at my birth my father wanted me to become the wife of a certain Gasana, the son of one of his friends, who he admired greatly and who had helped him out in the past, or something like that.

We rarely take on our fathers' names. Our names reflect the will or hopes of our parents, sometimes even conjuring up a curse. 'Habyarimana' means 'fathered by god'. 'Kakuze', 'we hope he'll grow up', is the name of a child whose parents lost the previous child. 'Jyamubandi', 'may you be welcomed by the other children', designates the love child of a woman whose husband knows how to forgive. A father may name a child 'Munderere' as a sign of reverence for the mother. It means 'raise this child for me', implying: 'because you're the best wife and the best mother there is.'

The missionaries used to assign us first names, simply taken from the Christian calendar. You're born on 5 February? You will be called Agathe; 28 June? Irénée; 3 September? Grégoire. If too many children born on the same day are baptized together, more exotic names are found, such as Janvier, Juvénal, Zachary, Théoneste, Anaclet, Évariste, Onesphore, Théobald, Athanase, Callixte, and Tharcisse. Being baptized is a calling card. No baptism, no first name. Without a first name, you have no social status. Those without first names are pagans, or sons of prostitutes. In Rwanda, baptism is a means of social climbing. Nearly every Rwandan then has a Christian name and a Kinyarwanda name. The missionaries were completely fooled, thinking they had converted us because we bent our language towards the Eucharist.

If only they knew! Rwandans have their own opinions about Christianity. We know how to soften up the priests, performing the Catholic rites with enthusiasm. But in secret, at night, we sometimes conduct traditional baptisms in honour of Imana, and pray to the ancestors. Such celebrations are denounced by the priests, and if found out, communion is denied until the whole family goes to confession.

In the east of the country, the mindset is still very pagan. People believe in zombies and spirits who travel in gourds. One day my brother Nepo even showed us a gourd haunted by a soul in the road. The fruit was moving from side to side gently and zigzagging at random. We watched it, some unbelieving, others worried. Until Nepo pulled a frog out from inside!

I'm in the midst of telling Eugénie this story when there's more thunderous knocking at the door.

'It isn't the Interahamwe,' says one of the other women in the room. 'It's Jérôme. I saw him from the window.'

Eugénie turns to me.

'Jérôme? Jérôme! Hide under the table!'

From the enthusiasm with which Father Vanoverschelden greets Jérôme, I can tell that he's the best of Christians. He's the head of the core ecclesiastical community in Nyamirambo parish. To the priests he's almost a saint. Twice widowed, he finally devoted his life to being a religious minister, albeit without orders. He knows the whole parish, he knows the births, which baptisms to conduct, what funerals to prepare for. Jérôme is the priests' right-hand man. But...

'Silence! Here he is!'

Jérôme has a soft, almost singsong voice. 'So my Father? Are you still as worried?'

Father Vanoverschelden explains that since the massacre in the church two days ago, the women are anxious.

'Completely understandable, Father.'

Silence.

'What are you going to do with all the Tutsi women you're hiding?'

'Tutsi women? We're not hiding any Tutsi women. We're only hiding innocent Hutu women.'

'So there are no Tutsis here? You're lucky! Because I heard the Interahamwe say that they'd even kill you priests if they found out that you were hiding Tutsi women here.'

Silence.

'Are you certain there are no Tutsi women here? Tell me the whole truth. I can protect you.'

Jérôme enters the hall like an unwelcome visitor and continues: 'You see, my Father, because of my position I'm able to reassure the Interahamwe. If you have complete confidence in me I can help you.'

'No, there are no Tutsi women in the parish.' Father Vanoverschelden's tone is formal. 'I only offer shelter to hungry women and to orphans. That's all.'

They turn to endless banalities, then Jérôme ends with this sermon:

'Father Vanoverschelden, I'm doing everything in my power to limit the massacres. I swear before God that I hate the Interahamwe killings and I love the Tutsis as much as the Hutus. Are we not all Christians? And was it not your former colleague who baptized me? Eh! How could I renounce the beautiful Christian faith?'

The two men embrace and Jérôme leaves. The front door closes after him with a crash, and beams are placed across it.

'Well, he's still a decent guy,' says Father Vanoverschelden. 'Why did you hide?'

Eugénie explodes: 'Why? Because Jérôme is a traitor! The only reason he comes here is to find out whether you're hiding Tutsis. And if he discovers you are, he'll be quick to tell the Interahamwe and they'll come to cook their prey.'

'You're wrong, Eugénie, you're wrong. Jérôme is a good Christian. He came to find out how we're doing. He is a little curious, that's all.'

'That man is a traitor. You alone, Father, are taken in.'

'Jérôme is a saintly man. I won't let anyone speak ill of him.'

I jump to my feet, drunk with anger. 'I couldn't care less whether he's a saint or not, you're not to reveal that I'm hiding here!'

'But Jérôme would be happy to hear that you're hiding here. I just didn't want to tell him without asking you first. I trust Jérôme, he's our best Christian, in any case better than you, Yolande.'

Father Vanoverschelden meets my gaze with dark eyes that seem to ask: 'Why didn't you take communion?'

He turns on his heels and leaves. Eugénie gets back on top of her table. She glances at the school out of habit then turns to the roadblock. Jérôme is talking to the Interahamwe. They're laughing and drinking beer. She can hear them.

'Muganga isn't with them,' Jérôme says, laughing. 'I'm sure of it. But I'll find her, I promise you.'

There's no midday meal, for a good reason: there's nothing left to eat. The afternoon begins with the torpor of tropical heat. Children cry. Women sing nursery rhymes softly to try and send them to sleep. The word 'hunger' is on everyone's lips. I don't want to leave the dining room where mass took place. Not because I like it here but because I'm afraid of being surrounded by distrustful Hutu women.

Emmanuelle has called the priests. She said she'll come to collect me from the parish: how, she doesn't know yet. She told the priests to prepare half a pound of beans for her that she can use to explain her journey at the roadblock.

'Hola! Cockroaches!'

The angry shout is loud enough to reach our ears. Like victims who need their executioners, Eugénie and I get up onto our table again to see who is talking to us. Even though they can't see us, the Interahamwe yell insults and threats to make us anxious.

'Apparently there are pretty girls among you. Give them to us and you'll be free.'

That evening the priests decide that all the girls in Mu Bwiza must shave their heads to make themselves look ugly.

I sleep with the women nobody wants to rape.

Early in the morning I hear cries and whistles. I get up silently and perch on the dining-room table. A child is running along the road, chased by ten or so militia men. Others block the road, catch him and take him back to the roadblock. I hear blows of a hammer and then the sound of a coconut cracking as his skull explodes. So this is the sound I heard under the sink at night! The Interahamwe weren't thirsty; they were executing people.

'Have you heard what we've just done to the baby snake?' shout the Interahamwe. 'It's what we've got in store for you. You'll be our dessert.'

Unbearable laughter. Why don't they kill us straight away? No, that would be too quick, unsophisticated. Death must first be accompanied by its cortège of agonies and suffering.

The next day, two militia men approach our windows with their radio blasting. RTLM: a certain Valérie has the microphone...

'Remember that we have only one enemy, the Tutsi. Some of them have swapped their identity cards between themselves. Don't be fooled by their papers. Look at their physiques. Remember that a snake is good at hiding. He could be anywhere. Think of everyone you saw in Parliament where the rebels were based during the Arusha talks. They were doubtless taking them milk, because all Tutsis drink milk. Don't spare anyone, above all not the children. Don't forget that the rebels attacking us today were babies when they left the country. Some were still in their mothers' stomachs. Don't forget, iyo uhetse impyisi ikurya amatwi, you can't carry a hyena on your shoulders without it eating your ears. He who spares even one Tutsi life is carrying a hyena on his back.'

The diatribe is followed by a military tune that the Interahamwe often hum, and then another litany against the Tutsi, to which the soldiers respond: 'Well said! That's the truth! Death to the cockroaches!'

Father Vanoverschelden calls me aside discreetly. 'Emmanuelle has just called with a plan. She'll come to get you this evening around five o'clock, with some soldiers.'

The idea of being taken away by soldiers doesn't fill me with hope. What if it's a trap that Emmanuelle hasn't figured out?

# 20

've been given yet another name. Emmanuelle hands me a Hutu identity card.

'From now on you'll be called Nyiraminani Alphonsine. And you'll be our aunt, mine and my sister's.'

I glance outside. I see a four by four with a white interior. A soldier is at the wheel, beside him is a female soldier of some rank judging from her epaulettes.

'She's your sister?'

'Yes. She's called Murielle. She won't hurt you. But I beg you, play along.'

Murielle gets out of the vehicle, comes towards me and clutches me firmly.

'You don't have anything compromising on you?'

'No, nothing.'

'Sure?'

'Yes. No! An empty pack of cigarettes I've been using to write down a few dates.'

'Give it to me.'

'Why?'

'Give it to me.'

I undo the knot at the edge of my cloth, and the packaging falls to the floor. Murielle crumples it up and throws it into the small bank of rose bushes. I have no more records.

'Now, let's go.'

At first we try to make the women inside believe that the soldiers have come to assassinate me. It's a precaution to dissuade them from trying to come with us, which might give us away.

One of them begins to cry in earnest. Did she love me then? Or is she crying for her own likely death and that of her child?

As soon as we're outside, the game changes. Now we have to pretend that I'm Murielle's aunt so that the Interahamwe at the roadblock will let us pass. I make an effort to walk like an old woman, to shake and stumble over my cloth. Murielle holds me up by the left arm; in her right hand she holds tight to a submachine gun, ready to fire if things go wrong.

'Don't worry, Yolande, I'll take you to my superior. Even though he's a Hutu and a Colonel, he has agreed to shelter you because he knows you a little. Besides, he's a man from the South; he knows that his own skin isn't worth much more than yours.'

'What's his name?'

'Colonel Rucibigango.'

I freeze.'What? Rucibigango? But he's a brute!'

'No, Yolande, he's not all bad. You've got to know how to deal with him, that's all.'

'I'm not going! Take me back to the priests.'

'We can't go back, it would be suspicious.'

I storm: 'This guy has AIDS, and he runs after everything that moves. You're sending me to my death! Just three years ago he tried to seduce me. He even came to see me at the clinic from time to time and bought me beers.'

'There's no other solution! The Interahamwe suspect you're hiding in the parish.'

'This guy is a bastard! Is passing on HIV his way of taking part in the genocide?'

'Be quiet.'

I send Emmanuelle a despairing look. 'Surely you're not going to leave me in the hands of Rucibigango!'

But my words have run dry and no longer come out of my mouth. I don't have any strength left to defend myself. I do what I'm told on automatic pilot: I'm the old village woman they're asking me to be.

'Come on, get in!'

I obey. The Interahamwe have watched our row with an unhealthy interest. I realize that I've made a mistake. We set off, but the Interahamwe stop us after fifty metres. They don't even look at photographs or peoples' faces; they're obsessed with three pen marks on the identity card. At least one of these marks must cross out the word 'Tutsi', printed next to the words 'Hutu', 'Twa' and 'Naturalisé'. They check again and again as we pass through thirty-odd roadblocks.

Oh my Rwanda! My unrecognizable Rwanda!

I know every detail of this road into the centre of town. And yet, I don't recognize anything. This is the first time since Habyarimana's death that I've been able to properly observe the area during the day with something resembling calm.

The trees to my right have all been cut down. People say they were hiding Tutsis. Fields have been burnt. Dead cows are rotting where they lie. Houses have been destroyed, some in part, some completely. On the walls you can see bullet holes. A roof shows scars from a fire.

To my left is Mount Kigali. It seems to have been spared. Suddenly, I see ten or so corpses, abandoned on the road. From then on, we pass an almost unending line of bodies as we get closer to the centre of Kigali. Sometimes we have to zigzag to avoid disturbing the dead. They all look alike: mostly men, half naked, with red marks where they were hit: the forehead, the nape of the neck, the heels, the arms. Some are still breathing, even with their foreheads cut wide open. From time to time, I make out a woman in the pile, her overturned basket a little further on, empty. Then there are the groups of children, four or five young boys, their arms cut off as they tried to protect themselves. Another woman has her knickers around her ankles; raped before being killed, no doubt. In the sky, clouds of black kites flutter and glide, looking for food. Further on we frighten away a whole group of them; they've been feeding on twenty-odd bodies.

A dog pulls at the cut-off head of an adolescent girl, one of her plaits in his mouth. I look on stupidly. 'That's one thing that won't happen to me,' I say to myself, 'I have hardly any hair left.'

Abandoned cars, burned, turned over. Bodies in the gutter, bodies arranged in a line to make a barrier, bodies the

Interahamwe, and even children, are still laying into. I see one child attacking a dead body with a machete too big for his age. He seems to be enjoying it. We hear groups of men singing. One man dances on the tarmac, applauded by the idle onlookers.

And at every roadblock, we go through the same interminable ritual. We present our papers, and the men chatter between themselves, seemingly disappointed that we're Hutu. If we were Tutsis they could kill us!

At one roadblock, a man explains to an adolescent how to handle a machete: 'You have to lift it up really high towards the sky while holding on tight to the handle, and then you cut them down with a sharp blow.'

The adolescent practises on a woman lying on the ground, whose chest is still shaking with the force of her convulsions. With the first blow he succeeds in cutting off her hand. He turns towards his teacher and smiles, drunk with pride. That's why there are hands, arms, feet and legs scattered on the road.

People are carrying fridges, beds, mattresses, household appliances, and more, pillaged from the homes of dead Tutsis. The stronger ones carry roofing sheet metal and even bricks.

The Interahamwe militia man is the same everywhere. He carries a machete in his right hand, and in his left, a portable radio glued to his ear, the antenna shining in the sunshine. He signals for us to stop by holding his machete out horizontally; waves us away with his machete like a policeman; greets his friends by raising his machete. It's as if it has become inseparable from his arm, it's now a natural extension.

Those without machetes have knives, axes, clubs decorated with nails, or sticks. They walk past the bodies, without bothering to finish off those who are lying there in agony. Some of the bodies are in a state of advanced decomposition. They give off a strong smell sometimes you can even see the skull, whitened by the sun. I say to myself that must be the Tutsi smell. I think I'm going mad again. I experience a sudden resurgence of the desire I've fought back before: the desire to offer myself up to the executioners. I want to jump out of the car crying, 'Tutsi! Tutsi!' so that everything will be over. Do I hold myself back simply because I don't want to betray Emmanuelle?

In some places, at the risk of their lives, people have thrown blankets over those who are not yet dead. Do they come back the following night to move the blankets from those who have died to those who aren't dead yet?

A bulldozer pushes twenty or so bodiest owards a ditch, where they fall, one after the other, as if there's order in this apocalypse.

My mind empties completely. I feel like a road-accident victim being taken by ambulance to an unknown hospital. I no longer react at all. I simply let myself be pushed around without asking any questions.

Not far from the military camp in Kigali, our car turns towards a housing development, climbs a small hill and enters a garden. I'm with the Hutus now; at the Hutu Colonel's home. I'm at the heart of the genocidal machine but a heart that kills, not one that gives life.

I still have a card to play. I hardly know this Colonel, but I know him enough to defend myself, and to get around him. Ah Colonel, since I'm in your grasp, here's the game I'm going to play with you. I'll behave in a nice friendly manner. It will look like we know each other so well that your staff will think you're hiding a member of your family. And if you threaten me, I'll use this tender family connection as a way to take you with me to the dead. That will make you think twice, perhaps.

I construct my plan in the time it takes to get out of the car and enter the house. I will it to work with every sinew in my body.

# 21

At the end of a long journey, when a village woman reaches the house of a respectable man, she leaves her luggage in a corner and walks towards him, head lowered, holding up her right arm with the left and offering her hand as a sign of respect. When I enter the Colonel's house, this is what I do. He is sickly and so puny he seems to float in his own clothes.

He smiles cynically and greets me, showing that he knows me. 'My condolences, Madam. We've cut off your breasts.'

My blood runs cold; he means that my children are dead. How could he know? And what if it's only a way to make the soldiers he's chatting with believe that I'm a Hutu woman, married to a Tutsi, whose children have been executed? My voice chokes but I'm strong enough not to cry. He's waiting for my tears, his lips parted with a hyena's laugh.

'As for your husband, we can all replace him satisfactorily.'

I want to throw myself at his throat, dig my nails into his eyes. But I can't betray myself. I smile as if I appreciate his humour.

The Colonel is an ugly man, around fifty years old. His small black eyes reveal his meanness and vice even more clearly than his words. He's someone you'd send packing if he came to court you, but he's a Colonel in the Rwandan Armed Forces; he could have you executed straight away. He clicks his fingers and dismisses the soldiers around him. The only one who remains is a certain Charles, a tall beautiful man I haven't met before.

'Would you like a beer?'

Charles serves me a beer that I don't touch.

'Charles here was in the midst of telling me about his work. Go ahead, continue your story.'

'So, my Colonel, I swore in front of all of the soldiers that if just one of the cockroaches escaped I'd leave the country for good because it would confirm, once more, the theory that we'll never succeed in exterminating all the Tutsi.'

These words enter my body like daggers. The Colonel seems amused. There's no doubt, he's trying to terrify me. But why? Charles continues, very pleased with himself:

'Habyarimana was a very intelligent man. Imagine, he constructed a plan that would succeed even after his death! May he rest in peace. We'll never have such a great head of state again.'

I feel attacked on all sides. Emmanuelle and Murielle lower their heads. They can feel my helplessness. But, no! I'm not helpless, I'm infinitely sad. And at the same time, proud. Charles continues in the same vein. He brags about having killed ninety-nine cockroaches.

'I only need one more to be able to have a break!'

Am I that one? What if this is nothing but a trap I've walked straight into? I stop listening, and the faces of my three children pass before my eyes. They smile as they meet my gaze. I remember the way Nadine came back to find me when we were separated, how she hugged me in the hedge for the last time and told me to be brave. Where are my children?

I'm startled by my father's name. Charles sniggers.

'The daughter of Ngenzi, a certain Consolata, was picked up by Shyanda's local authorities near Butare.'

Consolata, my sister! He has no idea he's talking about my sister!

'She seemed like a complete fool! She asked the policemen innocently: "Does the mayor know about my arrest?" "Does he know about it? He's the one that sent us!" The fool! A machete blow helped her understand in the end.'

Charles laughs heartily. I count my dead. Since the start of the genocide I've lost my husband and two sisters: Hilde and Consolata, and who knows what's happened to Nepo. Where are my children? Charles continues, excited by death, enjoying himself, twisting the knife. And I think: Nahungiye ubwayi mu kigunda, I've fled the dirt by hiding in the bush. Things have gone from bad to worse. The Colonel notices my disgust. Perhaps he decides the game has gone on long enough? He plants his little black unblinking eyes on Charles and says in a sententious tone:

'What if the Hutu are being manipulated by those in power?'

As quick as lightning, Charles understands the cue. He must stop talking about the massacres. A few moments later he gets up, excuses himself and disappears.

Emmanuelle and Murielle lay the table. The house is modern, richly furnished. I look at the buffet, the flowery plates, the cups, a small blue vase. Next to the fireplace is a large ebony statue of a naked woman, beautiful, slender, her arms stretched out as if she is just waking up from a wonderful dream.

We dine in almost complete silence. I can't eat anything, I can barely manage a cup of sugary tea. I feel like a fly drowning in a jug of milk.

Murielle chooses this moment to discuss my fate:

'If you agree, Colonel, tomorrow I'll take Yolande to Butare. She can pass as a member of my family there.'

The Colonel listens distractedly.

'Send her to Butare? That's not a bad idea. But not to your family.'

He has slid a hand under Murielle's shirt. He coughs coarsely, wipes his phlegm on his trousers. As if Emmanuelle and I weren't present, he feels Murielle's breast gently. She doesn't dare react but her eyes meet mine. I understand she's powerless, she has to bend to the Colonel's will. Top officers in the Rwandan Armed Forces have certain 'lordly rights'.

'Why not with my family?'

'It's dangerous. Even your family isn't safe, seeing as your mother is a Tutsi.'

'Perhaps.'

'Perhaps', said before a superior officer, means 'yes'.

It seems I'm the only one of us four who knows that my sister has been killed. Nobody else has made the connection between Charles's story and me. But I wonder whether the Colonel isn't in the know, if Charles's words weren't a masquerade designed to throw me off guard. Maybe they're in league together? But to what end?

I take a shot:

'On that note, Colonel, don't you think that it would be a good idea to make people think that I'm your aunt?'

'My aunt? Haha! You're not stupid, are you? I can see you coming, this is a ruse so nobody will think you're Tutsi!'

'No, not at all, Colonel, nobody will think that *you* are protecting a Tutsi!'

He scratches his stomach dreamily. 'Well –'

A phone call ends the dinner abruptly. The Colonel shows us a bedroom and disappears into the night. We are alone at last. Murielle begs me to be wary of her superior.

'He says white one day, and black the next. I'm sure he's plotting something. I know him too well. Don't celebrate your victory just yet. Yolande, I swear that in my family, nobody has blood on their hands because we know that bloodshed brings misfortune. So I'll do anything to save you, but you have to be doubly careful with the Colonel. He's a formidable enemy. If he gets it into his head that he wants to make love to you, you won't be able to escape him. You know he's HIV positive, don't you?'

'Yes, and I noticed his cough. It's typical of lung problems linked to AIDS. He must already be seriously sick.'

We go to bed. Kigali is nothing but a torture chamber of a thousand hectares. All night long I hear cries, whistles, machete blows, bursts from automatic weapons, grenades detonating, gunshots, and sometimes the long lament of a woman, half-dead, abandoned somewhere.

The Colonel returns with company and they drink beer, laughing loudly in the sitting room. Why hasn't he killed me yet?

All night long I turn various solutions around in my head: killing myself, giving myself up at a roadblock, hiding under a lorry headed for Zaïre, hiding in the false ceiling here, and so on, each idea more absurd than the last. I even imagine I'll squeeze myself into a jam jar and Emmanuelle will carry me to Uganda. I no longer know whether I'm sleeping, dreaming or delirious. I try to imagine the blade of a machete on the nape of my neck, hoping this game will make me less afraid when it happens, tomorrow perhaps, or in five minutes. Then come the regrets: Why did I leave the bush? What could I have done differently? If I'd let myself be felled by the Interahamwe in Nyamirambo, would my children have been spared? Are they dead? Who saw them die? No. It's not possible. My children are still alive.

At breakfast, the Colonel tells us he has decided to go to Butare with Murielle and Emmanuelle to take stock of the situation. He'll leave them there, then we'll see about my transfer later. That's it, I've understood. He wants to make love to me here, freed from these two women who are with me all the time. I'm such a fool! I see why he humiliated me yesterday evening. He wants to put me completely at his mercy, to make me so full of despair that I give myself to him without a struggle.

What a strange seducer's pride! What a pathetic attempt! I laugh to myself. 'So, Colonel, you're just a wretched little third-rate seducer? You have so little confidence in your charms that you court me with humiliation and threats? You'll see who Yolande Mukagasana is!'

Now I feel like I've grown wings, I'm almost joyful that I've regained my weapons.

Emmanuelle drags me from my thoughts with sobs in her voice:

'Colonel, Yolande can't stay here too long. You go with Murielle, I'll remain and tomorrow morning we'll follow you. What do you think?'

He looks at her, taken aback by her daring, coughs a little, then gets up ceremoniously. He concedes drily: 'As you wish!'

With his fists clenched, he marches off without eating, then calls Murielle. We hear the car pulling away. Emmanuelle has been truly courageous. She doesn't know that she ruined the plan I'd been constructing, so I can't reproach her for it.

The Colonel returns. Three days pass and I've still not been raped. He tries to seduce me by giving me a little portable radio, stolen from one of his victims no doubt. His sexual allusions become more explicit. I know that if I give in, tomorrow I'll be dead.

Emmanuelle bears the brunt of his bad mood. He hurls abuse at her, snubs her daily. I listen to the radio in secret and dream of putting my plan into action. But it would endanger Emmanuelle; she'd pay for it with her life. I use the telephone when nobody's around and hear that a friend was killed with her baby on her back. The Red Cross managed to evacuate the child.

The climate becomes even more stifling. The Colonel changes tack and takes in two other girls, from who knows where. Is he trying to make a point? The four of us can't sleep in two beds, I'll have to get into the bed of Monsieur, the coughing Colonel? Or is it all about letting Emmanuelle know that she must leave for Butare? Well then, I'll have to put my plan into action with Emmanuelle here, but without letting her in on it.

# 22

When the Colonel isn't at home, the soldiers come and go as they please. They eat the meals at the house prepared by the Colonel's cook, a barely trained new recruit. Sometimes they bring back a fridge, which they sell off right away for next to nothing. Perhaps they are suspicious of me because one day they show me a microwave oven and ask me what it is. I pretend to have never seen such a thing; I even feign fear, which makes them laugh.

'She's such a fool!'

I hear them talking among themselves regularly.

'Do you remember the girl from the Ministry who walked past every morning without greeting us? A secretary, quite a pretty girl –'

'The thin one with the gold glasses?'

'Yes, her. Do you know what happened to her?'

'No.'

'Well! This morning she came to me in tears. "Save me, save me!"'

'And what did you do with her?'

'What did I do? My military duty, of course! I asked for her papers. I saw that she was a Hutu, but I had my doubts. You know, she's quite a tall girl. So I interrogated her. She got scared and finally confessed that her father is Tutsi. You can guess what happened next.'

'What did you do?'

'I called her a cockroach. I told her she was nothing but a snake who'd taken the place of a Hutu. And I put a bullet in her head. You should have seen. All the passers-by stopped and started insulting and kicking her.'

'You shouldn't have killed her straight away. You should have denounced her first, let people beat her up, and then finished her off.'

'You're right, you're right. But I was so furious at having been deceived for days by the fact that she worked for the Ministry.'

The two soldiers slap each other on the back.

'In any case, all's well that ends well.'

'It will all end badly,' says the cook, out of the blue. 'Three days ago, in Kibirira, a woman dipped her fingers in the blood of her murdered son and flung it on the killers, cursing them.'

'And what happened to her?'

'She was killed then and there. But beware. All this spilled blood will bring us misfortune.'

'Spilled blood will bring us misfortune? You're not a Tutsi, are you?'

The cook shrinks. No, he's not a Tutsi, he says, but he's afraid of Imana's vengeance.

The soldiers laugh. 'On the contrary, Tutsi blood brings good fortune! All those who have spilled blood in the past are ministers, ambassadors, and the like, today! Eh! I can see you haven't shed any Tutsi blood, otherwise you wouldn't be a cook!'

'Imana is the sole judge!'

'Imana! Imana! You're too funny! When did Imana last look after Rwanda? That's the army's job now.'

'You know, little one, I'll tell you something. If Tutsi blood brought misfortune, my father would have been dead long ago. In Kibirira back in 1973, he shed hundreds of litres of blood, and rightly so. He tied up Tutsi men, women, children and threw them into one of the rivers that feeds the Nyabarongo. And you know where they ended up, those bodies? They were carried by the current all the way to the Akagera and, they floated peacefully towards Lake Victoria, and on to Ethiopia, you understand? For the first time in history, the Tutsis went back to what was once Abyssinia, a place they never should have left! That was my father's work. And it seems to me it didn't bring him misfortune, since he's still alive, and he's as tough as a tree!'

The cook looks at the soldiers with the air of a schoolboy who's learning the sum of two plus two and is amazed but doesn't understand anything.

'And Imana? Won't Imana be angry?'

'You know what happened in Kibeho, little one?'

'Something happened in Kibeho?'

'Yes! Imana sent his mother there and she appeared to a student. It seems she was even a virgin.'

'The student?'

'No! The mother of Imana. They say she's a virgin.'

'But how can she be a virgin if she has a son?'

'Listen, child, it's too complicated to explain. But I'm telling you that the Virgin, mother of Imana, appears regularly to a student.'

'And this student, is she a virgin?'

'I wasn't there to check! You're getting on my nerves with your idiotic questions. I'm telling you that the Virgin appears regularly in Kibeho. And you know what she said to the student? She said that President Habyarimana is in heaven, that he's been assassinated by the Tutsis, and that, to revenge his murder, all the Tutsis must die. That's what the Virgin said.'

The cook can't believe his ears. 'What's her voice like? Is it gentle?'

'Nobody can hear her voice except the student. That's the sacred mystery. But we can hear the student, that's how we know what the Virgin says. You understand?'

'Not really. But it's a magnificent story.'

The soldiers laugh at the cook and ask him to fetch them some beers. They still have seven houses to go over with a fine-tooth comb before nightfall.

Sometimes the soldiers address me sharply. 'Where are you from?'

'From Butare.'

'What are you doing here?'

'The war took me by surprise. I was bringing presents for my daughter who lives in Kigali. Then the President was killed, and my daughter fled to Europe.'

'Why did she flee? Was she afraid?'

'She was married to a Belgian. They left at the beginning of the massacres.'

Over the next two hours, I embroider a cock and bull story about how and why my daughter fled that the soldiers listen to attentively. She escaped across the Gashora marshes in the south east of the country, not because she didn't like the Hutu, because she was a Hutu, but because her husband, a courageous good sport, was implicated in the murder of three Tutsis. In collusion with Hutu extremists, he had invited some Tutsis to join him for a drink in a bar, the extremists entered all of a sudden and the Tutsis were cut to pieces. But he was unlucky: a neighbour denounced him to the police and that's why he fled. And so on... My imagination surprises me.

Little by little the banana beer has its effect on the soldiers, they lose all suspicions and we even have a good laugh about the misfortunes of the Tutsis. They're half-drunk by the time the Colonel returns late that night. They stand to attention and then disappear immediately to nurse their beers under a banana tree.

The Colonel is tired. He's come back from a tour of the country. He flops into an armchair with gloomy eyes.

I ask perfidiously: 'Would you like something?'

'A whisky, dear.'

I run here and there. A whisky? Where is the alcohol? Where are the ice cubes?

'I feel terrible!'

'I'm coming, Colonel.'

'Don't call me Colonel.'

'What should I call you?'

'Call me Alexandre.'

In this strange house I manage to lay my hands on the three essentials: a glass, whisky and some ice cubes. I present them to him submissively, like a servant girl.

'Yolande, I'm an unhappy man. Shame on me, my dear.'

The little Colonel is slumped in an armchair. He coughs for a while.

'Yolande, I'm dammed. I'm a dammed man. And I have no more hope.'

He drinks the first glass in one go. I fill it up straight away.

I kneel before the Colonel, leaving a respectful distance so that his hand can't reach me. There is a long silence. I look at his boots, stained with earth and blood. Tutsi blood!

'Yolande, I don't understand this war, I don't understand anything. I'm so alone! What are we doing?'

'What *are* you doing?'

'We're killing Tutsis for no reason. With no real motive. Ah! I'm so tired! What a fate!'

It's too easy to invoke fate. Does fate have arms long enough to reach down to earth and wield a machete? It's too easy to say that you're just a cog in a machine, that this is beyond your control.

'I'm just a puppet. Someone else raises my arm, puts a machete into my hand and brings it down on innocent people.'

Silence, while we look at each other. No! We examine each other, spy on each other, we devour each other with our eyes.

Is this man really suffering? Or is this his latest trick?

He has a third glass of whisky.

I want to say: 'Look at me, Alexandre. Look me in the eyes.' Alexandre? So in my thoughts I'm now calling him by his first name, Alexandre. Didn't he ask me to call him Alexandre to build trust between us?

Either this man is of the devil, or he's sincere. I tell myself: Yolande, you planned for this so you have the advantage here. You hoped for this familiarity, now you have it. But be sure you know what you're doing. This man is HIV positive.

'Alexandre, Alexandre, we'll come out the other side of this!'

Alexandre looks at me sadly. His gaze says: 'You'll come out the other side of this, perhaps. But it will be without me. Me, I've got AIDS.'

He slides a hand under my cloth with purple flowers, and caresses my breast mechanically, like he does with every woman. I know that he doesn't really want me; for him seducing is a habit. We stay for a long moment sitting side by side on the sofa. I despise Colonel Rucibigango, but I pity Alexandre. Or am I fooling myself with my own plot? No, I must go for it, he'll drink a little more and he'll be off my hands.

He belches. 'I've killed countless Tutsis. I'm guilty. I like killing them. I feel pleasure when I kill them. I'm a coward. I don't know what's got into my head. I'm like a madman. Yolande, I love you.'

The Colonel is drunk. Clumsily, he falls to my knees. I look at him, indifferent. I want to say: 'You love me? Ah well, tough!'

I've won the first round, but the price is feeling compassion for my enemy.

I help him to his bedroom, where he collapses onto the bed, and then I return to Emmanuelle's bedroom. I don't tell her anything. I feel even more alone.

I spend the night contemplating the curious feelings a victim has for his or her torturer. Is it pity? Is it disgust? Is it a mixture of both? And why is it impossible to get away from the idea that the torturer is a human being?

How should I interpret the Colonel's confession?

# 23

I t's the morning of the fifth day, or is it the twelfth day, or the fifteenth, I don't know anymore. It's the morning of the day that everything goes wrong.

Outside, the war has intensified. Kigali is drowning under an endless rain of shells. The Rwandan Armed Forces are fleeing. The Interahamwe don't even ask for identity cards any more: a quick glance is enough. If you look Tutsi, that's the end.

The cook catches me listening to Radio France International and reports me to the soldiers.

'I swear she understands foreign languages! She's a spy.'

'A spy, are you sure?'

'Yes. I'm sure!'

'Thank you. You're a good chap. So, what shall we do?'

'To the roadblock,' replies another soldier.

'But what if we're mistaken? They say the Colonel respects her.'

They whisper among themselves for a good fifteen minutes. I can hear footsteps all over the house. Should I jump out of a window? But where would I go? At best, I could hide in the garden. Emmanuelle has a stroke of genius. Instead of falling to her knees and praying as usual, she goes straight up to the soldiers.

They shout at her: 'Who is this old woman who speaks foreign languages? She was caught listening to the radio.'

'The old woman?' Emmanuelle feigns surprise. 'But she's the Colonel's aunt!'

'What are you talking about?'

'Yes, his aunt. Eh! But I can see you don't believe me.'

'Well she's just a village woman – why is she listening to foreign radio stations?'

'That makes complete sense: she's lived nearly all of her life with foreign nuns, in a convent near Kibuye.'

'She's not married then?'

Emmanuelle bursts out laughing. 'Married? You must be joking! She's a spinster! Nobody's ever touched her, she has no children at all.'

The soldiers laugh wholeheartedly. 'A silly old spinster!'

'You know, she's a bit soft in the head too. And bitter. You must understand, for forty years, she lived with white nuns, serving them. And then suddenly, when the President was assassinated all the nuns fled, flown out by MINUAR. They abandoned her at the convent without a thought, without even saying goodbye. There are women who would be driven mad by less.'

A soldier peers backwards to take a look at me through the doorway with disgust.

Emmanuelle adds, 'Can't you see how dirty she is? She hasn't bathed since Habyarimana's death. She promised God not to wash herself until all the Tutsi are dead. Just look at her bare feet, brown with dirt.'

'She'll soon be able to wash herself,' replies the soldier. 'Soon there won't be a single snake left in all of Rwanda.'

But the other soldier remains suspicious, and asks Emmanuelle to call me.

'Mukecuru! Mukecuru! Come here a moment.'

*Mukecuru?* The way a young person addresses a woman of a respectable age! I approach, pretending shyness.

'What radio were you listening to, Mukecuru?'

'The one my nephew gave me.'

'Yes, but which station?'

'I don't know.'

'Where's your radio?'

'I'll fetch it.'

On my way back, I have enough time to turn the dial before handing it to him. When he turns it on only a crackling sound comes out.

'What did the radio say?' The soldier asks me.

'The radio? The radio?' I play the fool for a moment as I think of what to say. I can't talk about the advance of the Patriotic Front or they'll get angry. 'It said the massacres will soon be over because there are almost no Tutsis left.' A sufficiently vague statement that could come just as easily from RTLM as from RFI or the BBC.

'And what do you think about that?'

'I think the nuns will soon be able to return to the convent, and then everything will be just like it was before.'

The soldier hands the radio back, declaring that I'm even more backward than most country women. 'I bet she didn't even know what she was listening to!' The others laugh loudly, and call for the cook to bring them more beer. Emmanuelle and I smile discreetly. Once back in our room, Emmanuelle kneels and thanks God.

Still, we must to do something. The advance of the RPF on Kigali is making the soldiers ever more nervous. One of these days they may just kill me in a fit of rage. And perhaps Emmanuelle too.

Ah! If only I could put my plan into action now! But the Colonel isn't frightened enough yet. I know there'll come a time when the Patriotic Front is enough of a threat to make the government soldiers fear they've lost the war, even though they won't admit it. That will be the time to act. If I move too soon, the Colonel will kill me out of anger. If I act too late, he'll kill me out of spite because he'll have nothing left to lose, sure that he's going to be killed anyway in an RPF strike.

Every evening, when he comes home, the Colonel elaborates at length on the magnificent work of his troops sniffing out snakes in fake ceilings, in the bush, even inside wells. His crisis of conscience from the other night is forgotten. His 'I'm guilty!' – forgotten. I wonder, is he rotten to the core? He kills, or at least gives the order to kill Tutsis across the whole country, while simultaneously protecting me in his own home. Is he a fool, the devil, or just a man pulled between two poles of conscience? One, his duty to his government, the other, a moral imperative against gratuitous murder. In this genocide there are two radically opposed ways of being. In front of his conscience, man bows down and respects the lives of others, ready to deceive his fellow fanatics. But in front of the fanatics, the soldier in him comes to the surface once more, revelling in the pride and glory to be gained from killing. That, no doubt, is the genius of those who prepared and orchestrated the genocide. They have somehow managed to lobotomize the killers so that many are able to go out and kill diligently, like automatons, then come home from work and become good family men once more. And you, my little Colonel, floating around in your clothes, are you still tugged between these two poles?

I've taken to asking the Colonel what he thinks of the RPF advances. He replies, 'The RPF don't have any logic, Yolande, they attack a hill, bombard it for ten days, and then instead of taking it, they disappear. There's no understanding Kagame's officers.' Every evening he repeats the same observation, laughs uproariously, and then coughs. What he forgets to say is that five days later that hill is covered in soldiers from the Front. Nobody knows how they got there, nobody saw them coming, but now they're in charge of the hill. They detain the Interahamwe and soldiers from the Rwandan armed forces, catching some as they kill civilians, in the act of committing genocide.

I read the Colonel's moods with care to know when the time is right. But every evening, when he arrives home, his voice sounds too in control, too cheerful. I'm watching and waiting: I know that one evening he'll come rushing back and stumble over his words. The mighty Rucibigango will be no more than a child crippled with fear.

For now, I'm reduced to listening to the news from the RFI and the BBC in secret. I learn that Sindikubwabo's government fled to Gitarama, then further on to Gisenyi, on the border with Zaïre, opposite Goma. I hear the Patriotic Front is advancing on almost all fronts, and that they've surrounded Kigali. Actually, I hardly need to be told that: true to their tactics, they're bombarding the town daily. How much longer can this last? A week? Three days? Or tomorrow will I wake up to the *Song of Arusha* being sung in the streets? Tomorrow, will I see RPF soldiers on the road outside? Maybe tomorrow morning I'll be able to slip through the window to safety. I go to bed nursing this dream, murmuring the Front's favourite song: 'We've succeeded, we the brave. In Arusha, they praise us with songs. We've succeeded, we who did not fear death.'

I press myself against Emmanuelle. 'I want to live, Emmanuelle, I want to live.'

But she's asleep, a rosary between her hands.

# 24

Our hill has become a target for the Front. I'm woken by shells falling all around us. An artillery battery must have been set up on Mount Kigali or one of the neighbouring hills, because we're bombarded non-stop. Outside, the district is on fire. I hear the Colonel get up, call his aide-de-camp, and issue orders in a nervous voice. His car pulls away at breakneck speed. The first phase of my plan has come to pass without me having to do anything: the Colonel is unsettled. The second stage is to isolate him. The third, humiliate him, and the fourth, make him sing. But patience; everything in its time.

Emmanuelle's bulging eyes are almost as awful as mine. She's crying and moaning: 'It's the end, Yolande. We'll never get out of this alive. Listen to the cannon fire.'

With every detonation her body trembles. She wants to hide under the covers, then under the bed, then in the garden. As for me, I'm not disturbed by the blasts – they've become so familiar. And besides, what does it matter if I die? Actually, no. I don't want to die, but I'm not afraid of dying. Is this what serenity is?

Dawn is swift. In less than twenty minutes I can make out people on the road: shapeless columns of women carrying heavy bundles on their heads followed by a stream of children. Destination: exile. These Hutu women must believe the government radio stations who claim that the RPF soldiers kill everything they find in their path. Apparently they have long ears and rape all the women they meet.

I slip into the garden and crawl to the edge of the road. Twenty or thirty metres away, a roadblock operates its sinister sorting as per usual. A few Tutsi women who tried to seize this moment of general panic to escape are cut down. Their children run into the neighbouring gardens, where they're quickly found and finished off with machete blows. A shell explodes nearby. An Interahamwe has his arm blown off; he does a stupid dance, howls in pain and then collapses. He's abandoned on the spot by his luckier colleague who is too busy filtering out the remaining Tutsis. Reinforcements arrive. After pushing their colleague into a ditch with their feet, the three men begin to examine identity papers. It seems hunting Tutsis is more important than protecting themselves. From time to time, a small lorry or van passes by, and is loaded up with bodies.

I've seen enough and go back inside. Emmanuelle, rosary between her fingers and face turned towards the ceiling, resembles the Virgin Mary at the Assumption. Her lips move in prayer that she unwinds like a ball of wool. In response, I turn on Radio Muhabura, the rebel station. 'Hariya Arusha baraturirimba!' Finally, that song of hope! Now I know that I will be saved, now I know I will survive. It's not my time to die. But where are my children?

A newsreader explains the MINUAR Blue Berets haven't yet left, but they will in another five or six days. How to hold on for another five days in this hell? Next, a military song, then an interruption for a special announcement:

'The troops of the Rwandan Patriotic Front have taken Kanombe airport. I repeat, RPF troops have taken Kanombe airport. The government army soldiers are fleeing Camp Kigali in the centre of town. I repeat, Kigali airport has fallen...'

The news brings Emmanuelle out of her devotions. We hug for a long time, stroking and squeezing each other. I start to cry, never have I been so happy. I have rediscovered the tears I couldn't find in me to cry for my loved ones and now I can't stop.

We move to the sitting room where we can see, about two hundred metres away, part of the Camp Kigali barracks.

There's an incessant rush of lorries that we can just make out through the dust they raise. It's hard to see exactly what's going on. A bomb falls on one of the barracks, breaking through the roof as if it's a sheet of paper. I don't even spare a thought for the injured soldiers. All I can think about is that the difficult conditions I need to carry out my plan are now coming together. We'll be able to have breakfast in peace.

The two Hutu girls sit opposite us. I haven't spoken a word to them in three days. The bombing has got them scared although they don't know that the airport has fallen. It's funny; just yesterday, these two girls looked at us with disdain, pitying the village woman and her old-fashioned sidekick. This morning, the situation is reversed. The girls are out of their minds with fear. They ask if I'm afraid of the bombs. That's it! I know how to get rid of them.

I reply with irony: 'Me? No... When you're old, you're no longer afraid of dying.'

'Do you think we should flee?'

'That depends. But do you know what will happen if you don't flee?'

'No!'

'The RPF soldiers are brutes, they murder everyone in their path. And they're rapists; do you think they'll deprive themselves of girls as pretty as you?'

'So what should we do, Mukecuru?'

This mark of respect tells me I've reeled them in. 'Flee, my children. Flee.'

'But where to?'

'To Zaïre!'

The word Zaïre shocks them to the core. It means abandoning everything and becoming a refugee. One of those refugees dependent on the meagre funds of humanitarian organizations. I revel in their helplessness; their faces are undone. But still they resist.

'Perhaps the Rwandan Forces will regain the upper hand. Perhaps everything is not yet lost.'

I play my last card: 'Everything is lost, little ones. The RPF has just taken Kanombe.'

'Kanombe?' They are petrified.

'Yes, alas. But don't tell anyone, because that will discourage our soldiers. Keep it to yourselves and flee while you still have time. They say the rebels have begun to invade our hill.'

'But you, Mukecuru, aren't you afraid?'

'What do you think they'll do with an old woman like me? It's not as if they're going to rape me. I smell of rancid butter.'

'And Emmanuelle?'

'Emmanuelle has vowed to stay by my side until the last moment. She has a beautiful character.'

Emmanuelle lowers her eyes. She doesn't know whether to laugh or cry. The girls abandon their meal, disappear, consult each other in private and then return, one with a large yellow bundle, the other a red one.

'We've decided to leave. Thank you for your advice.'

Their goodwill almost embarrasses me. I wish them a safe journey. When they've disappeared, I hate myself just a bit for having tricked them, for having driven them into exile, but I didn't have a choice. If they were to witness the trick I'm cooking up against the Colonel, they'd take his side, and then it would be Emmanuelle and me against the three of them.

We finish our breakfast in relative peace. The shells exploding around us keep us tuned to the battle's progress. I imagine the two girls walking in the heat towards the West, their bundles on their heads. I can now put phase three of my plan into action, but must wait for the Colonel's return.

# 25

The day is spent watching birds. Mostly black kites, huge birds of prey with forked tails and wingspans almost a metre and a half wide. They move in flocks slowly across the Kigali skies, their whinnying cries clamouring above the city. Spotting something on the ground, they circle it, gliding for a good while before attacking their prey: abandoned bodies no doubt. A cannon shot sends them off towards a neighbouring hill in the beat of a wing, and from there they begin their approach tactics again towards a new target. Once they've eaten, they fly nervously in every direction disbanding into the sky. An hour later, they're back, or are they a new lot?

I think of the binoculars that belonged to my children – the ones the Criminology Department confiscated on the pretext that they were destined for the rebels in the war of October 1990. They would be useful right now. What if the Colonel has some? Quickly, Emmanuelle and I agree that I'll slip into the Colonel's bedroom while she stands watch. If anyone appears, she'll sing.

I tiptoe into the Colonel's bedroom. What a spectacle! It's teeming with military equipment. Around the bed are boxes filled with grenades, the more common type with a pin and strange ones that look like geometric mushrooms. On a shelf there's a brand-new pistol; I pick it up, it's heavy. In a box I find a hundred or so little phials that look like perfume samples, but must be some sort of poison. Under the bed, ten or so guns are lined up like branches in a woodpile. I continue to dig around and stumble upon folders filled with files bearing a red stamp 'Secret'. I read quickly.

    *– Operation BWA. Strategy to adopt in case of the destruction of bridge F 67 over the river G 7/7A.*

    *– Plan Alphonse. Recruitment of Interahamwe in the Save Sector, Butare Prefecture.*

    *– List of arms transfers since 3 April in the Prefecture of Kigali Town Centre.*

The files are in Kinyarwanda. They're dotted with code names, rendering them completely incomprehensible. I learn that in the case of J 786, B 89 must contact X 18 in the name of Sylvestre to launch Operation Avalanche the same day as Operations Karisimbi and Kilimanjaro. And then there's a list of people in the category A1, for the town of Byumba. I understand nothing, except that the genocide was well prepared because these files date from the months of January and February 1994, and, in the list of people in Category A1, I recognize the names of people I know, Tutsis.

I move to the cupboards and find boxes and boxes of bullets, a classified map covered in markings and arrows, and a pair of binoculars. I take them and return to the sitting room, then on second thoughts go back to take the pistol; if things go wrong, I'll kill myself. After leaving the bedroom for a second time I'm seized with doubt: what if the Colonel notices that the pistol has disappeared? I'll be done for. I put the pistol back in its place and instead slip a grenade into my underwear, lumpy like an enormous hernia. I make a decision: if my plot fails and I have no other solution, I'll set off this grenade in the Colonel's presence and we will die together. But what about my children? I haven't thought of them since... Since when? A week ago?

The theft has quickened my heart. I give the binoculars to Emmanuelle and shut myself in the bathroom. I take out the grenade and look at it for a long time. It's my only possession in a country where I've lost everything. Remembering what I've seen soldiers do in films, I find the pin and mime pulling it over and over again until the motion becomes automatic.

Then I tuck the grenade back into my underwear and rejoin Emmanuelle in the sitting room.

The window is our lookout post over the west of Kigali. With the exception of Mount Kigali all the neighbouring hills have been cleared of trees, exposing white stumps like amputations. Here and there, the remains of a destroyed house are being salvaged by children who transport bricks, balanced on their heads, along a path across the hill. Abandoned vehicles lie on every side, even army and MINUAR jeeps, with their gun carriages desperately naked, not a single machine gun left behind. These defenceless vehicles seem to symbolize the absurdity of the MINUAR mission: maintaining peace in the midst of war.

With the binoculars, I spot two vehicles about to pass each other. A MINUAR jeep stops for a moment on the side of the road, and as a Rwandan Armed Forces jeep drives past, the soldiers salute each other. Aren't they all Africans, after all?

The radio announces that this morning there are more than eighty people hiding at the Mille Collines Hotel. It's on the other side of the hill so I can't see it. Nor can I see the Church of Sainte-Famille, another place I've heard is filled with fugitives. I can't see the airport either, blocked by the Gikondo hill, but I do see the military camp, where there seems to be a rout. Vehicles come and go endlessly and shouted orders reach us even here. A good sign: it shows that the rebels are closing in on the city. But numerous buildings are still controlled by the government forces. So even if the rebels are drawing closer, the final assault is not here yet. When will the coup de grâce come? And will it come before the Colonel decides to give me up at the roadblock on the corner?

I turn towards the South and follow the line of electric pylons that runs along the little valley of Nyarutarama on to Nyamirambo. But however much I look, I can't see my house. I recognize the three cedar trees that grow near my clinic, so familiar in the Rwandan landscape, their branches sloping like Chinese hats. But my clinic is invisible. Black smoke rises a little further on; tyres burning at a roadblock.

Are my children still in the area? Are they somewhere over there, hidden in a banana plantation, or under a sink, or behind a piece of metal roofing? Or are they somewhere else, in Butare, in Shyanda?

The hours pass by unbearably slowly. On the radio I hear that Rwanda's troubles are headline news in Europe and America. A minister in the West has talked about the country's national debt, 'that Rwanda will need to settle one day'. Yes, Mister Minister, if a few of us survive the genocide, we'll pay you back for the weapons that killed us. I learn that the Hutus who pillaged houses of Tutsis are killing one another over the loot. I hear that supplies cannot enter Kigali because all the surrounding roads are in the hands of rebels except the road to Butare. I guess the RPF have left the government troops an exit route to prevent them from committing additional massacres out of despair.

As night descends swiftly, the clamour of a new flock of kites passes over the city like a storm. They seem to be decrying the city's state and terrible smell. They pass over the house, fly towards Mount Kigali, and disappear over the other side, taking with them their secrets, mysterious indisputable witnesses to the genocide.

# 26

The evening begins slowly. Hours pass as I wait for the Colonel to return. I turn on RTLM to hear the enemy's view of the situation. There's a song by Masabo. The cook, who loves Masabo as much as I do, comes running and starts dancing, clapping his hands. Let me find out more about this little cook.

'If just one Tutsi must be spared, little one, let that Tutsi be Masabo!' I say.

'Masabo? But he's a Hutu. They say he's doing his work well!'

Everyone has betrayed me, even Masabo.

The radio claims the airport is still in the hands of the government forces, that the RPF has been forced back, leaving dozens of their number dead. The cook celebrates, but I have my doubts. At this point the Colonel comes back, surrounded by three sergeants. He's clearly nervous.

'What is happening, dear nephew? You seem anxious.' I mask my mockery.

He gives me a black look, but his voice softens immediately. 'Nothing, nothing. Everything is going well.'

I can sense that he's lying. The news that the RPF is controlling the airport is burning my lips. I want to hurl it at him like a blow, but I'm not too sure after the latest RTLM news. Isn't it always the government's tactic to deny evidence until it is public knowledge? The thought calms me: yes, Kanombe airport must be in the hands of the rebels.

The cook has retired, there's nobody left to cook *monsieur* the Colonel's meal.

'Would you like to eat? Are you hungry? I could make something for you.'

The small man looks at me, his eyes betraying the gratitude of his stomach. As if they're giving a press conference, the three sergeants declare that they're also starving. My four enemies will be at the mercy of a great omelette that I'll liven up with tomatoes and sweet potato. Like an old mother fussing over her son who has become an important man, I serve whiskies to these warmongers with false enthusiasm. Emmanuelle follows me like a choirgirl with a plate of grilled peanuts.

The men talk about a faulty Russian-made mortar they found in a camp won back from the rebels. 'And you know, Colonel, next to the mortar was an abandoned hand. The charge must have exploded in the face of the person trying to fire.'

The four men laugh loudly, while I make sure their omelette is properly runny, the way the Colonel likes it. Emmanuelle and I follow each other in a small procession, me first, with the omelette and four forks in the frying pan held out like a sacred dish, and Emmanuelle behind me with the bread and spices. During a war, you don't serve onto plates. Even though they're famished, the sergeants have polite reflexes; they wait patiently for the Colonel to start eating.

'Serve me a little more whisky would you, Aunt? And some for my colleagues.'

The Colonel raises his glass to the glory of the rebel forces.

'The rebel forces?' cries a sergeant.

'Yes, of course the rebel forces! They are killing themselves so sweetly, and even leaving behind their mortars for us!'

More loud bursts of laughter as the omelette disappears under the fork attack. They tear at the bread in fistfuls. 'We're still hungry!'

I cook another omelette. I want to spit in the eggs as I whisk them but hold myself back because I know that this evening I'll have my revenge. Yes, I know it. After devouring the second omelette, they stretch out heavily in the armchairs.

I sigh loudly.

'You seem sad, Aunt? What's going on?'

'My nephew, I have some bad news. It seems that Kanombe has fallen into the hands of the rebels.'

My remark stuns them. The four soldiers look at each other without saying a word. Their distress thrills me. The Colonel coughs.

'How do you know, old lady?' asks one sergeant.

'The radio.'

'The radio?' The colonel looks aghast. 'It's not true,' he shouts. 'I've received no information about this. It can't be.'

'Maybe it's not true; these foreign radio stations report everything and anything.'

I'm glad to discover that Colonel Rucibigango is badly informed. Not that I'm completely sure of my information. 'In any case, it's certain the airport has been attacked.'

'It hasn't been attacked, dear Aunt, otherwise I would have been told.'

One of the sergeants breaks into nervous laughter. He says, 'In any case, we can't lose this war! Even if we retreat, the French will come from Central Africa to support us.'

Another responds: 'The whites helping us? You know as well as I do that they're always on their own side. If we lose, they'll abandon us.'

The sergeants raise their voices.

'We must win this war!'

'Oh yes!'

'You're sceptical?'

'I don't believe in it anymore.'

'You don't? Well, you're free to switch to the cockroaches' side if you want. But you'll regret it!'

The remark is so dry it provokes a long silence.

The discussion starts again timidly, but heats up as they broach other sensitive topics and burst out angrily with rude remarks. In the end, the sergeants salute their superior and retire, then the Colonel shuts himself in his bedroom. Their goodnights were glacial.

Emmanuelle and I head to our room too. As she prays, I take the grenade out of my underwear carefully and place it under my pillow. On second thoughts, if the Colonel surprises me in my sleep, I need to have it within reach. I replace it delicately in my underwear.

The Colonel doesn't sleep the whole night long. I hear his anxious footsteps, confirming that the third phase of my plan is taking shape. I wonder whether he's getting ready to denounce us at the roadblock before fleeing. I try to sleep but I can't stop thinking about the Colonel and this war. You can't fight several wars at the same time: you can't persist in killing Tutsis, in raping women, in looting houses and also sustain a war against soldiers armed to the teeth.

The next morning, breakfast is boarding-school fare: tea, bread, even jam.

Rucibigango looks at me eating: 'It seems you've regained your appetite!'

'Thanks to your good care, Colonel.'

'Do you know you're becoming a beautiful woman again?'

Here's the last weapon I need. The Colonel has had his eye on me; I knew that it was enough to rouse some anguish in him for his lust to flower again. He thinks I'm a pretty woman? Well then! I'll show him what a pretty woman is capable of.

'You're making fun of me, Colonel!'

'Not at all. I'm speaking with utmost sincerity.'

'I'm nothing but an old hyena!'

'Believe me, Yolande, you're a truly beautiful woman!'

I look at my plate, acting coy.

Two soldiers interrupt us.

'War, war, always the war! When will I be able to...'

But the Colonel stops himself, tells me he has to leave for the front line once more. 'When I return this evening I'll teach you two things. First, that the rebels were not able to take the airport. Second, that I know how to love a woman; something too deep to express in words.'

Underneath my clothes, his hand seeks out my breasts and squeezes them. 'Tonight, I'll make you a happy woman.'

He leaves. So tonight I'll be raped. Is that so? Ah, but Colonel, do you know who you're dealing with? It is I, Yolande Mukagasana!

# 27

I spend another day birdwatching. Kites are magnificent creatures. From time to time I take the binoculars and scrutinize the surroundings, but there's nothing to see, everything is happening in my head. Then I return to the birds, but I'm distracted. I'm only waiting for one thing: the return of the Colonel.

The government radio confirms the loss of Kanombe. I burst into laughter; the little Colonel's time is up. The third phase of my plan is coming together. The Colonel finds me beautiful? Well, he'll find me even more beautiful this evening.

'You're not really going to put on makeup!' Emmanuelle is stupefied.

'Why not? I'm a woman, aren't I? And I've recovered some of my health thanks to the warm hospitality of our Colonel.'

'But he's a monster, Yolande. He'll rape you! And you know he has AIDS.'

'Yes, yes, I know.'

'I don't understand you. Why carry a hyena on your back?'

I leave Emmanuelle to her proverbs and enjoy getting dolled up. And no, it's not just to seduce the Colonel, it's also because I've become a woman once more, a woman who likes to seduce.

'Pray, Emmanuelle. Pray that my makeup won't be useless.'

Instead of praying, she cries.

For three days, I wait for the Colonel who, I find out later, is on tour in the South. Three days of making myself up uselessly, except for the pleasure of the soldiers' gaze.

'Eh! You're not as old as you think,' remarks one of them. 'You're still beautiful for your age.'

So my work is having an effect. But what if it's too effective? What if, on his return, the Colonel throws himself on me and rapes me? I don't care. My body no longer belongs to me. I'm ready to let myself be raped if this will return my children to me.

Every evening, I wait for the sound of vehicles. The only ones that stop are with soldiers coming to get ammunition from the Colonel's bedroom. If he is dispensing his personal reserves in this way, no doubt the government forces are at the end of their resources. I caress my stolen army grenade every now and then, under my clothes, like a pregnant woman caresses her stomach. Sometimes I imagine the Colonel raping me: he tears my clothes, I unpin my grenade. I hold him close in a passionate embrace, and we die together in the explosion. That's perhaps what it means, to love your enemy.

Finally, the Colonel returns accompanied by two soldiers, both equally drunk, or are they high from smoking cannabis? Two young women tag along, but all they do is look down at their shoes. Perhaps the soldiers abducted them, to rape them later. The Colonel appears less drunk than the others.

We eat. The cook has succeeded in finding two chickens that he serves us with a creamy cornflour sauce, a real feast. There's joy in the air, but also death and fear. Each person behaves as if the world doesn't exist, as if Rwanda itself has never existed. Each time I raise my eyes, I meet the Colonel's gaze. The third phase of my plan is in motion.

'What are you going to do if we flee, my aunt?'

'I don't know. Why would you flee?'

'Because the airport has fallen into the hands of the rebels.'

'Ah! Really?'

'Don't play the innocent! It was you yourself who told me about it first.'

'Ah well! I'll stay here, I think.'

'Here?' The Colonel is taken aback. I'm speaking as if this is my home. 'But you'll get yourself killed by the rebels!'

'The rebels can't massacre everyone! Perhaps I'll escape.'

The Colonel is mad with anger. Not only is he obliged to let his soldiers believe that I'm comfortably at home in his house, but that I'm also refusing to follow him into exile.

'Well then, Emmanuelle will come with us.' He is more cunning than I thought.

Emmanuelle refuses, claiming that her legs are in too much pain and she needs urgent treatment. The Colonel, suspicious, dismisses everyone, declaring that he needs to speak to me alone. This is what I've been waiting for, but it frightens me because I have to play double or quits. Is my plan foolish?

'Come, let's sit in the armchairs.'

I obey and choose an armchair some distance from the sofa where the little Colonel has sat down. He gets up, gets two glasses and serves me a large whisky.

'You've got your strength back now. A little alcohol will do you some good.'

He comes to perch on my armrest and takes my hand. I offer no resistance, but I'm full of fear that I might not pull this off.

'You've got goose bumps. You're not afraid of me are you?

I shake my head, and squeeze the Colonel's hand with my own. That's it, Colonel, my infernal machine is en route.

'Yolande, you have lost everything now, your husband, your children, your house. But you mustn't let yourself be crushed. On the contrary, you should let people who wish you well come close. You are still young and beautiful. You could have many things in life, and even more children. I'm the first candidate on the list. I would like us to make a child together.'

His dry hand searches for the path to sensual pleasure under my clothes. I let him. I'm disgusted by his desire, I think of his AIDS.

'You please me a great deal, Yolande. I think I've shown you just how much by letting you stay here, at the risk of my own life, when Tutsis are being killed like rabbits and their wives raped. I'd like to sleep with you.'

A shell falls a few metres from the window and the Colonel throws himself to the floor. I look at him calmly and want to laugh. Colonel Rucibigango is afraid of shell explosions! Moreover, he's fallen at the feet of his future mistress, who didn't blink an eyelid.

'Let's go to bed!'

'Not yet, Alexandre, I have things to say to you.'

Calling him by his first name comforts him and gives him confidence. 'You are so beautiful, Yolande. I want you.' He has lost all self-control.

'Thank you for the compliment. I didn't know I was still desirable in this pitiful state. I don't know how to thank you for the great risk you've taken in keeping me here for so long. However, it's still a little too early, don't you think, to dream about remaking my life. You're an intelligent and civilized man; you can understand that I need time for my wounds to scar over.'

As I speak, I see anger mounting in his face. Good, he's been caught in the trap.

'I'm touched by your good heart,' I add, acting like a woman who has all but given herself, even as she says, 'not yet'.

I let his mouth find mine, I let his hands move over my body, I even pass an arm around his neck. With my other hand I undo his fly, plunge my hand inside and caress his member. Immediately, he gets excited and like a beast in full heat, abandons himself. I feel his hot semen on my hand. After a moment, I get up, and go wash my hands and my mouth; I'm afraid of getting HIV.

I hear the Colonel pacing up and down in the sitting room.

'You take me for an imbecile,' he shouts on my return.

'Not at all, Alexandre, not at all. Forgive me if I forced you; I only wanted to demonstrate my good intent. I'm not ready yet to make love with you but that will come. Maybe even tomorrow. I know that we'll love each other soon. I can feel it.'

My words calm the Colonel down; he looks at me almost with kindness. I kiss him tenderly on the neck and escape to my bedroom.

I find Emmanuelle praying. I burst into tears. 'I can't take it any more, Emmanuelle, I can't. I'm at the end of my tether. Tomorrow he'll rape me for sure.'

She takes me in her arms and comforts me, and I recover somewhat. Haven't I succeeded in setting up the first three phases of my plan? Haven't I succeeded in instilling fear into the Colonel's soul, isolating him from his Hutu girls, and humiliating him? All that's missing is to make him sing.

'Emmanuelle, we're leaving tomorrow for the Centre of Saint Paul.'

'But how will we get there? We'll be killed on the way twenty times over.'

'Listen, Emmanuelle, you choose. You come with me or you stay here.'

'If I stay, the Colonel will kill me for being your accomplice. I don't have a choice.'

'I know. They're all like madmen now. They've lost the war and know that their sole hope is flight. But they'll make the Tutsis pay the price for their defeat. So there's no other solution: we must flee.'

'But how?'

'Just trust me. You'll find out as I put my plan into action. Get up, get dressed, pack your things. We'll spend the night waiting. And if it all goes wrong, I've got a grenade that I'll detonate to end everything.'

'If you want to kill yourself, why didn't you do so earlier?'

'I don't.'

We stay up the whole night listening for any sound coming from the Colonel's bedroom, but there is none. The Colonel has fled his humiliation in dreams.

Contrary to my expectations, the next day he's in an excellent mood. He's relaxed, and even smiles at Emmanuelle, perhaps for the first time. He orders eggs, jam, bread, and sings to himself as he butters his bread. He asks if I've had a good night.

'Excellent, Alexandre. I thought about you all night long.'

The remark pleases him; he's really taken in by my game.

Two soldiers appear; they've come to take orders.

'Please, sit down, have a cup of tea.'

It's almost joyous around the table, we laugh and tell jokes about the RPF. I drink sugary tea and gulp down six slices of bread.

'It seems that the hope of building a new home has given you back your appetite, Yolande!'

I get up, unceremoniously. 'Excuse me, Colonel, but I'm making you lose precious time. I wanted to thank you from the bottom of my heart, before your very own soldiers, for having looked after us so kindly – Emmanuelle and myself – and for such a long time. But I don't want to take advantage of your kindness any more, and that's why we must say goodbye.'

The Colonel laughs nervously. 'You're saying goodbye? And where do you think you are going?'

'Emmanuelle and I are leaving.'

'You'll get yourselves killed on the street corner!'

'No, Colonel, we're leaving for the Centre of Saint Paul, where they say there are lots of people seeking safety.'

'But how will you get there? There are at least twenty roadblocks on the way and the buildings are encircled by Interahamwe. Ah! You make me laugh, Yolande. Perhaps you want to get there by helicopter? Well, I don't have one!' The Colonel rages on, even as he laughs heartily. He senses that something is escaping him, he senses some sort of trick. 'You will not leave.'

'But Colonel, you had the kindness to welcome me into your home for all this time, surely you'll also be so kind as to drive us under your own protection to the Centre of Saint Paul. If I'm not mistaken, it's on the road to Butare, so it won't be an inconvenience to you.'

'No! You're making fun of me. I'll never drive you anywhere.'

'Must I remind you, Colonel, that you don't know how to honour a woman who desires you?'

The two soldiers smile at each other discreetly.

'How dare you!' Rucibigango fumes.

'Colonel, enough of this chatter. I'm trying to save your life.'

'My life? Why would my life be in danger?'

'It's in danger, Colonel, because you don't keep a close enough eye on your telephone and confidential numbers. I called the chief commanding officer, General Bizimungu, on your behalf, and I told him two things: first, that I'm a Tutsi, and second, that I'm your aunt, but not just any aunt. I took care to clarify that your father is my brother, meaning that you too are Tutsi, Colonel. So, either we leave together for Saint Paul, or we'll die here together, at a roadblock, or even here in this room one way or another.'

The Colonel begins to shake. He begs. Why did the woman he was protecting denounce him as a Tutsi? 'I'm not a Tutsi. I'll prove it. I've got an identity card.'

'Do you think, Colonel, that I would have forgotten to tell the chief commanding officer that your identity card is fake?'

The little Colonel is beaten and boiling with anger. Yes, he will drive me to the parish of Saint Paul, but on condition that I telephone the High Command first to tell them that I was lying.

'I'll call them from the parish, Colonel, not before reaching the parish.'

A long silence follows. The two soldiers don't understand what has just transpired. They murmur between themselves.

'Silence, you two! Get the car ready.'

The soldiers leave the room.

'Yolande, are your bags ready?'

'I have no bags, Colonel. Nothing.'

The Colonel's chauffeur drives like a madman, beeping and flashing his lights. The Interahamwe hastily step back from the roadblocks and salute the Colonel by raising their machetes. I recognize a dozen or so militia men, some of whom were close family friends. We reach the Centre of Saint Paul and the Colonel lets us out of his car. Safety, finally.

'Swear to me that you'll call the High Command and set the record straight.'

'But I have nothing to swear. I don't even know their number.'

'But, but then... then you lied to me –'

'On that note, Colonel, I need to give you back this grenade. I believe it belongs to you.'

# 28

**A**m I safer in these church buildings than at the home of Colonel Rucibigango? Nothing is less sure. But at least I'm with friends.

Saint Paul's compound is near the city centre, not far from the Mille Collines Hotel. The Centre and Church of Sainte-Famille form a religious complex run by the Pères Blancs, the Missionaries of Africa, who are black for the most part. The buildings are scattered across the property: to get from one to the next you need to be out in the open, where the Interahamwe at the entrance can taunt you, pretending to take aim with their sticks. On the far side, the grounds adjoin the bush, where huts made from branches covered with blue tarpaulin have flowered among the trees. In them our enemies take refuge, Hutus chased from the north of the country by the advancing RPF troops. They're armed with guns and grenades and fire at us from time to time. Although we're only separated by a simple hedge, they don't carry out a full-blown attack. The mystery of the weak-willed bully is unfathomable.

The Colonel drops me off at the entrance, where there's a roadblock. I go down the slope towards the first building with trepidation, expecting a bullet in the back. I don't dare turn around. With relief, I cross the threshold and glance back. The Colonel has waited for me to reach safety before leaving; that explains why the Interahamwe didn't dare attack me. Is he so evil, this little Colonel that I humiliated and forced to dance to my tune? Why did he keep on protecting me after all the tricks I played on him? Does he love me a little?

The registration of new arrivals takes place in a compact office. A small priest with skin as black as coal takes notes. 'Nyiraminani Alphonsine, 39 years old, Hutu ethnicity.'

'Yolande, Yolande, you're still alive! Everyone says you're dead!' A child all but jumps upon me in greeting. A friend of my daughter Nadine! I look at her with wild eyes, realizing that I no longer know how to smile.

'Where is Nadine,' she asks, 'where is Nadine?'

'Nadine? I think she's been killed, little one. But I'm not sure.'

The child lets go of me, wavers, and falls faint at my feet. Three women come running and look after her. The priest explains that Geneviève has been greatly disturbed since her parents were killed before her eyes as she hid under a car. I picture her parents; we had dinner at their house just a few days before the start of the genocide. Joseph and I with our three children.

The child comes to, looks at me uneasily, and shows me her jumper. 'This is Nadine's, she lent it to me.'

'Keep it, little one. You need it more than she does.'

I look at the child and try to smile. But no, I've forgotten how to.

The small priest interrogates me. Am I called Yolande or Alphonsine, he asks.

'Alphonsine, my Father. I don't know why this child thought I was called Yolande.'

'You seem to be in good health. What skills do you have?'

'I'm a nurse.'

'A nurse! Well then, you can help us receive new arrivals. Get in touch with the doctor here, put yourself at his service.'

'What will I have to do?'

'Every day, around fifteen new people arrive, and five or six others are killed, so that makes nine extra people, give or take a few. You'll need to find blankets, and look after the provisions.'

The priest's pragmatism scares me.

The people who have sought refuge here suffer from a range of problems: diarrhoea, malaria, fever, chills, pneumonia.

Every day the Interahamwe peruse the list of arrivals. Sometimes, without saying why, they take one or more of us away and attack them in plain sight at the roadblock guarding the Centre. 'It's to make an example,' they say, 'so that you know what's waiting for all of you!'

'As for you, Emmanuelle, you will help Alphonsine with all her tasks.'

The priest is astute enough to notice the sway I have over Emmanuelle. He disappears and Emmanuelle and I look at each other. She smiles.

'The Lord will protect us. I'll pray.'

The Lord! I'm fed up with the Lord! I've had enough of Emmanuelle's prayers. All I want to do is hide in a corner somewhere out of sight. I'd like to be looked after; I don't want to do anything until the RPF get here. But look, they're burdening me with duties as if I haven't suffered enough, as if I don't have the right to a *holiday*.

My revolt fizzles out. Still, I don't want to be Muganga any more, someone who looks after others. I'd like to be some kind of fool that people take charge of and who lets things be done to her. But no, I'm Muganga. I've become Muganga once more, she who cares for others and listens. I sense that I'll have to learn my profession again. Not how to give an injection, but how to love others, how to listen, how to wish them well, how to want to ease their suffering. For five weeks I've been hunted like a beast: from antelopes, I learned the art of hiding between hedges; from snakes, the art of hiding under stones; from foxes, how to pretend; from hyenas, I got a taste for biting those who wish me well. Now I must learn how to feel again. I must become a human being again. But do I want to?

I enter the large parish hall and a tide of malnourished children rushes to me. There must be at least a hundred people in the room. The Chinese whispers have moved faster than my feet; everyone already knows that I can treat the sick.

'Can't you give me a moment to get changed?'

I pull off the children clinging onto my clothes and go into a dark adjoining room. A child glues his cheek to the doorpost and watches me putting on my jeans under my clothes. I'm back in my combat clothes: trousers and a T-shirt.

I find the doctor and realize I know him: we took a course together three or four years ago. He's operating on a child with a wounded arm.

'You diagnose. I'll treat.'

'But doctor, you're reversing roles. It's your job to diagnose.'

'I don't have time to diagnose. I'm operating. You're Muganga, I believe? So diagnose and send me the worst cases. Work fast. We're overrun.'

I look at the man, flabbergasted. There's something fascinating about his pragmatism. I obey and call out to the room of sick and dying people: 'Who has a fever?'

Thirty arms go up. I make the women come up one by one. I listen to their lungs by placing my ear against their chests, gauge their blood pressure with my fingertips, estimate their temperature by sliding my hand between their thighs. Without any tests, using my experience and intuition, I diagnose malaria, dysentery, harmless flu, and a considerable number of pneumonia cases amongst people who hid in the marshes for weeks. I scribble the name of each patient's illness on a small piece of paper and give it to them to take to the doctor for medicine, if there is any.

A woman tells me she has been raped so many times she can no longer sit down. She has a fever. I examine her vagina. Generalized infection. Even her anus has been affected, it's full of pus. She won't survive. On her piece of paper, I simply write 'antibiotics'. No, I don't have the heart to tell her that she'll be dead in a few days. To me, she's already dead.

Children arrive, most with clear cases of malnutrition, but nothing serious. Fevers, swollen stomachs among the smallest, shivering, all that is routine. A newborn is dehydrated, I order a woman who has just miscarried to give him her breast. A child of five comes closer and begins to suck on the other breast; that's what hunger does to you.

Sometimes people arrive with wounds. A bullet has entered the breast of one woman and come out of her other side. By a miracle, no vital organ was touched. The bullet skimmed past all of them without causing any damage. I recommend antibiotics and two dressings, where the bullet went in, and where it came out. Can one be more logical?

'Do you think my baby will live?'

'Your baby? No problem.'

Before I know it, night falls. I cover myself up with a blanket that Emmanuelle holds out to me. Colonel Rucibigango is already far away.

'Emmanuelle, I feel so alone tonight.'

'You're not alone, Yolande, you're still able to offer some good to those around you.'

'I offer it in spite of myself!'

'That's what's beautiful about you: you do good without wanting to. Remember the words of Christ on the cross. He would have liked the chalice to pass by his lips.'

But I'm already sleeping. Who is this Christ?

# 29

The genocide has the power to obliterate memory. I no longer know whether I've been here for three days, two weeks or ten years. All I know is that I struggle day after day for my own survival and for the survival of those I treat.

At night we sometimes hear fights in the Hutu camp, often over goods stolen from Tutsis. A gunshot usually puts an end to the quarrel. One more death for a fridge or a cooker. The displaced Hutus have nothing in common with us. They're free to come and go, they're there only because they don't have money or a house to go to. Their life isn't in danger, except from illness. That said, they have weapons and seem to kill on a whim. They're getting more and more anxious as the rebel forces approach and the prospect dawns on them that they may soon be real refugees, threatened with death in their turn, or worse, being called to account for their crimes.

From time to time, to distract themselves, they hurl abuse at us, throw stones and sometimes take a pot shot. A few days ago a woman died from such an attack, which made them laugh a lot. Humiliating defenceless people exorcizes their fear of seeing justice turn against them. Or do they act out of despair, knowing that all is lost? Tomorrow, the luckiest among them will be in exile, while the others will have to pay for their crimes. Eh! Since they've already lost everything, what does one murder more or less matter?

I no longer know whether I'm a Tutsi, I don't even know whether I'm a woman or a wild animal. Perhaps I deserved these humiliations. I don't know: when you're humiliated repeatedly, you end up accepting your own humiliation.

There are almost two hundred of us here inside the Centre, piled up in every corner of the buildings. We sleep in the offices, the parlour, the chapel, the kitchens, even in the larders. Emmanuelle, as if by instinct, went straight to the chapel, where she contemplates with fervour a large Christ, made out of wood, whose neck has been cut but not completely broken by the Interahamwe, during one of their visits. It seems he is the God of the Tutsis.

Between the church of Sainte-Famille and the Centre of Saint Paul, there is a communications network worthy of the best postal systems in the world. You write a word on the wrapper of a packet of cigarettes for the attention of X, who can be found in the church. You give the word to Y, Y gives it to Z, and Z gives it to X. X replies on a sugar packet, and his missive reaches you within two hours. This is how I manage to reach a young man I know. He tells me about Father Stefano, a priest we see from time to time, who carries a revolver in his jeans belt. This man of God spends his days with the Interahamwe talking about the coup and drinking beer. He pretends to protect the Tutsi but gives them up regularly to the militia, one by one. Sometimes he rapes a woman he finds to his taste. One day, I don't receive a reply from my young friend. That evening, I learn that he has been executed.

The next day, a distant cousin of Emmanuelle brings her two little orphans, his cousins, at the risk of his life. He can't look after them because he's a soldier. The two boys seem to be in good health. I look at them and find my smile again. I still know how to love. Thank you, my two little ones, for giving me that. I take the risk of not registering them. There are so many children here now that the Interahamwe doesn't bother counting them all. I look after these two children all day long, but I cry sometimes between smiles: where are my own?

The next night, I hear two discreet knocks on my door. We quickly hide the children under the bed.

Emmanuelle whispers: 'Hide yourself too, Yolande.'

'No, you hide. I'm not afraid.'

Once more two discreet little knocks. This is not the way the Interahamwe announce themselves. I open, almost serene.

'Muganga, you have to help me.'

It's a large woman of about thirty. I recognize her, she's the daughter of neighbours in Nyamirambo. We've crossed paths a few times here, but I pretended not to recognize her to save her from embarrassment: she is unmarried and pregnant.

'Yolande, do you recognize me? I'm Martine, you were friends with my parents. When I was little you let me climb onto your back, remember?'

'Yes, I remember.'

'I'm pregnant. At the beginning of the massacres a militia man hid me in his house and raped me every night for two weeks. He raped me after work, with his machete still wet with blood. As a result I began to bleed.'

'Yes, I know all that,' I say, to cut the explanations short. 'What do you want?'

'When he saw me bleeding, he told me to go and die with the other cockroaches, that he didn't want an abortion in his house.'

I hear in these words the solitude of the Rwandan woman. No, I don't feel pity. I'm simply aware of the loneliness of women in my country.

'Martine,' I say to her, 'I'm tired of being Muganga. Everywhere I go, I'm asked to look after people. I'm fed up. There are other doctors in the Centre, go look for them.'

Martine begins to cry. She begs me. She trusts only me, she says. She wants to choose her doctor, possibly her last doctor before she dies.

As a way out, I tell her I have nothing to use to examine her.

'That doesn't matter, Yolande, I know you're a magician.'

A magician? Somehow the flattery sways me and I agree to help her. We leave together, slipping silently between the buildings, zigzagging like soldiers entering an enemy town. It's more dangerous to go out at night because the Hutu shooters are invisible.

Luckily, Martine's room is next to the priests' bathroom and they are away, no doubt busy with people in the chapel. We enter the bathroom like thieves, and Martine puts a folded scarf in the sink.

'Get undressed.'

She undoes her two cloths then takes off a big wool jumper, navy T-shirt and underwear. I examine her. She's become an enormous girl, filling up the bathtub. I don't know where the devil she has found all these kilos. Judging by the skin on her thighs, they're not from her pregnancy. I diagnose a miscarriage.

'You're going to lose the baby very soon.'

'I've already lost it. Look in the scarf in the sink.'

I unfold the scarf and find a foetus only ten centimetres long. From the atrophied umbilical cord, I can tell that the placenta hasn't yet come out. I turn towards Martine, who lies in the bath like a stuck elephant.

'I believe I can save you, but I warn you, it's going to hurt a lot. And you know that you can't cry out, because you'll draw the priests' attention.'

'I know. Do it. I hope I don't infect you; the militia man may have been HIV positive.'

I wash myself with soap and water and begin to remove the placenta with my hand. Martine's fingers grip the side of the bath, but not once does she cry out. Not even a moan. I clean her out thoroughly and put the placenta in the scarf with the foetus.

Martine has already got up behind me. 'Yolande, you must survive so that you can always be a doctor. Don't worry about my child, I've got a plastic bag and I'll find a way to dispose of everything.'

With these strange secrets, I return to Emmanuelle and my two orphans. I have a funny feeling. I've been irritated that people were still calling me Muganga: I had the impression people were taking advantage of my skills. But at the same time I'm aware that I've been able to do some good; I've saved this woman from a serious infection. In return, I've received something from Martine: the honour of dignity regained. And for the first time since the beginning of the genocide, it strikes me that I'm not the only Tutsi in Rwanda.

The next day, a crazy rumour spreads through the Centre. People are saying that the RPF and the government forces have reached an agreement about prisoners. The Tutsis in the zone still controlled by the soldiers can be exchanged for the Hutus encircled by the rebels. Everyone will be able to go to the opposite zone, where they'll be protected. The news provokes a mad joy in the compound: people talk about nothing else, they're almost dancing. But in the afternoon we learn that the first exchange couldn't take place because the Interahamwe blocked the road and stoned those who wanted to leave. Two hours later, we're told that a convoy of thirty-four Tutsis managed to cross the front line in the very centre of Kigali and join the rebel forces. So at least thirty-four Tutsis have been saved. They may be all that remains of my people.

News continues to flood in all evening, contradictory and incomprehensible. A convoy was gunned down in full sight of the UN Blue Berets who did not react. Two other convoys arrived at their destination near the airport. But the tension mounts. It seems that the Hutus given up by the rebel forces are setting to work again killing the Tutsis encircled by the government forces. It could all tip into carnage. Emmanuelle prays.

The next day I learn that the manager of the Mille Collines Hotel has been repatriated to Brussels, or somewhere, and that he's been replaced by a friend of mine. The French government has got the soldiers to agree that they won't attack people who've taken refuge at the hotel. I ask a doctor to alert the new hotel manager to my presence here at Saint Paul's.

'You can go out, can't you; you're Hutu, no?' I ask him.

'Is it written on my forehead, perhaps?'

I want to say 'yes'. I say 'no'.

The doctor makes three trips to the hotel, only about four hundred metres away, but each time he returns empty-handed: the manager can't be found, but an employee took a message.

I begin to despair. Things seem to be getting gloomier. We haven't seen any evacuation convoys; we almost stop believing in this fantastic possibility. Women burst into tears unexpectedly, at their wits end, scared by every gunshot. And I've also started to feel fear again. As if I have too much hope to be resigned.

The afternoon is long and dull, brightened every now and again by some reassuring news. But we don't believe the half of it and end up arguing endlessly about what's really happening.

All of a sudden the chapel falls completely silent. The women begin to shake and one hides in a confessional box. I turn towards the entrance. Am I seeing death? Standing in the doorway is a large officer with a revolver flanked by two soldiers armed with submachine guns. Everyone lowers their eyes waiting for the burst of automatic fire that will end our plight.

'Muganga Mukagasana Yolande.'

The officer pronounces the three words loudly as if he is haranguing a crowd at a meeting. An electric current shoots through my body. I fall to the floor and hide my face in Emmanuelle's clothes. For a second time, even louder, my name rings out in the chapel.

'Muganga Mukagasana Yolande.'

The tone is authoritative. Nobody turns towards me; they pretend not to know me. If I don't give myself up, I will risk the lives of all these people. What to do?

The third time the soldier shouts out my name, I break free from Emmanuelle's clasp. I've made my decision. I will get up and walk towards the officer.

The last six weeks of flight pass before my eyes. I see myself in the bush again, at night, and the obscure silhouette that passed a few metres away from me. I see Côme the militia man's beaming face again, and the way he swung his bottom as he walked in step with the soldiers. I see the grenades hanging from André's pockets. I see Joseph's severed hand and his death. I am in Spérancie's house again, surrounded by my three children like the Pietà. I see Déo's suspicious frown. I see the sink under which I spent eleven days. I see the Interahamwe smashing a child's skull and hear it exploding. It's as if it is my own skull that's cracking.

I try to get up, but my legs fold up under me and I fall heavily. I try again and walk with trembling steps towards death. I stand a few metres away from the officer.

'I am Yolande Mukagasana.'

I stop shaking, I'm resigned. I'm waiting to receive a full magazine of submachine gunfire in my stomach.

'You are Muganga Mukagasana Yolande?'

'Yes, that's me.'

All of a sudden, I become proud again. I straighten up and look the officer right in the eyes. I know how to die.

'The manager of the Mille Collines Hotel has sent me to find you and escort you to him.'

'Excuse me?'

'I've received an order to take you to the Mille Collines Hotel.'

I don't understand. Am I already in heaven?

People begin to whisper among themselves. I recover from my surprise slowly.

'I can't leave without two children and my niece.'

'What's the problem? Bring them, damn it!'

I ask myself whether it's a trap to get me executed. But how would a government soldier know that I know the hotel manager? Emmanuelle gets our clothes together in a hurry. Some are wet: a woman gives us a plastic bag. I haven't quite recovered. The world has turned upside down: I'm being saved by a government soldier, moreover one who is agreeable, even likeable.

I turn back to everyone else. I don't dare say anything, but I'd like my eyes to offer some solace.

'I'm happy for you, Yolande!'

I recognize the woman who has spoken; she came to my clinic six months ago. I smile at her but my throat remains tight.

Outside, there's a double-cabin vehicle, with two African Blue Berets leaning against it.

'Please get in,' says one of them. He points towards the exposed flatbed behind the cabin. I'd be too easy a target for isolated shooters.

I gather up all my English. 'The boys will go there. They will not be killed if nobody recognizes me.' Oh my! I've forgotten all my English. But the soldier understands.

'You are very clever, you know!'

So we cram ourselves into the cabin, with Emmanuelle lodged between the driver and the officer in an intimacy she's never known. I sit behind them, my head hidden on the knees of a Blue Beret. Behind, the children, flat on their stomachs, are protected by the other soldier who looks about him, as alert as the President's bodyguard. When we reach the hotel, the children get out first. When they're safely inside, it's Emmanuelle's turn, then mine. The MINUAR soldier puts his beret on my head and it covers half of my face, hiding me from idle onlookers trying to see who we are.

Once safely inside, the soldier takes his beret back and salutes me. 'Take care!'

'Thank you very much.'

The hotel's lobby looks like it's been devastated by an earthquake. There are clothes strewn around, sacks of flour, boxes of potatoes. Eight black leather sofas have been pushed together to make large beds. The shutters are closed and all the chandelier light bulbs are broken.

Then I find myself face to face with Spérancie, my niece Spérancie.

'Spérancie! What are you doing here?'

We hug, we cry.

'And my children? Do you have news of my children?'

The question chills the room.

'What? You don't know?' Spérancie lowers her head.

I know what I'm going to be told.

# 30

'**D**o you remember the day you fled to Déo's house?' begins Spérancie. 'That day, the Interahamwe came back, this time with soldiers.

'We had hidden in the kitchen. They order us to get completely undressed. Everything we are wearing belongs to them, they say. They take us to join two rows already formed on the road, one of naked women, the other of naked children. You are the only person from around us who isn't there.

'They push us towards a ditch that has been dug two hundred metres away. Everyone is naked but no one is embarrassed by their own nakedness, only dazed and humiliated.

'Your son, Christian, heads the procession. He begins to pray and invites us all to join him. He prays so passionately, it seems he's no longer with us. We all, without exception, chant responses. Christian takes on the voice of a messiah, talking about the next world, telling us to have courage. He says we will be able to love those who are our enemies here on earth. All around us, the Interahamwe seem drunk with the murders they are about to commit. They run from one end of each line to the other, mocking us to our faces, laughing at our distress.

'"Be brave, Spérancie," Nadine says. "Now that they're focused on us, maybe Mama will be able to escape."

'We reach the ditch. The Interahamwe are more and more excited. They shout at us, insult us and spit in our faces. The two lines are sent to either side of the ditch.

'"If anyone can tell me where Muganga is, he or she will be spared," shouts a militia man.

'Nobody knows except us four. But what use would it be to denounce you, since they're going to kill us anyway!

'"So? Nobody knows where Muganga is? Really! Nobody? What a shame! If that's the case, all of you, take a step forward so that those in front will fall into the ditch."

'We obey like machines. Christian steps forward first. A man rushes over and begs for mercy: "Please, spare the children of our benefactor. Muganga is good to all of us, and treats the poorest for free. She has always looked after everyone without any distinctions. I beg you, spare —"

'A gunshot interrupts his plea, the man crumples, and a militia man pushes him into the ditch before he hits the ground.

'"Let this man be an example to you all. Every Tutsi must be killed, be they a child, an old man, a pregnant woman or an invalid. This was our late President Juvénal Habyarimana's plan. And now, to work!"

'A machete falls heavily on the nape of Christian's neck, his head is cut three-quarters off, and he falls into the ditch. I leave the line and throw myself at the feet of the militia man directing the operations.

'"I beg you, kill me straight away! I don't want to see Sandrine and Nadine die! Muganga is my aunt."

'But one of the Interahamwe begins to shout: "No, that's not her niece, she's just one of Muganga's employees. Besides, I know her father, he's Hutu."

'"Then give her back her clothes," says the leader of the Interahamwe, "she can go."

'"No. I won't leave!"

'But it's useless. The Interahamwe carry on as if I'm no longer there. Sandrine's head is cut off in the same way as Christian's. When Nadine reaches the edge of the ditch, she throws herself in before they can strike her. While the other bodies are falling into the ditch one by one, we hear Nadine's muffled voice:

'"Goodbye, Spérancie, goodbye. Tell Mama, if you see her, that we are all dead. Tell her to flee as far as she can, far enough that nobody will be able to kill her. Perhaps she'll survive, or she'll die of sorrow. Tell her I'm afraid of machetes and prefer to die of suffocation. But tell her that I'm so afraid of dying."

'"You're afraid of dying?" shouts an Interahamwe. "Eh! But all you have to do is tell me where your mother is."

'"Why should I tell you? Even if you let me live, how could I want to live without Mama?"

'The Interahamwe, disappointed with Nadine's response, become angry and accelerate the rhythm of their work. Bodies continue to fall, one after the other.

'Nadine becomes delirious: "Mama, Mama, where are you? Mama, I'm scared. I want to dance. I'm afraid, Mama." Little by little, Nadine's words come less often. She begins to suffocate under the weight of the bodies. I remain there, dazed, until I can't hear anything else, then I stumble away. I am mad, empty, exhausted. I feel alone in the world. I wander across the countryside. All of a sudden, I realize I'm carrying my clothes in my arms; I'm still completely naked.

'There, Yolande, that's what happened. But I don't understand. Emmanuelle told me she'd told you.'

'I knew, Spérancie, I knew. And I didn't want to know. I knew that very day. I even felt the precise moment of their death in my body. Emmanuelle waited for nightfall to tell me because she was afraid of what I would do; she thought that I'd give myself up at the roadblock, and the Interahamwe would kill her too for hiding me. I sensed the moment of my children's death, because, in the midst of all the whistles and gunshots that morning, I felt my children calling me for help. I had cramps in my lower stomach and wanted to push, like you do when giving birth. Then I saw my mother as if in a dream. She was crying for me. She said to me: "Be brave, my child; he who has raised a blade against your children will feel a blade on his neck." My father was there too, and they both consoled me. They told me to live. I asked them: "But why are you crying for me?" They didn't reply. Before disappearing, they told me that everyone was watching over me. I asked: "Who is watching over me?" But they were already gone.

'You know, Spérancie... when I was hiding under Emmanuelle's sink, almost suffocating, so very afraid, I dreamt of my son, but just once. He was singing in a mass for the sick, and he touched my shoulder. I turned around and he smiled at me, but he didn't say anything.

'On the evening Emmanuelle told me that my worst nightmare had come to pass, I didn't want to believe her, instead, I pictured all three of them: my daughters dancing, Christian reading a comic book in his bedroom. But I must have known the truth at some level because my first reaction was an all-encompassing rage. It's true: I wanted to go to the roadblock and fight with those cursed killers who had just exterminated my whole family. I was ready to run wherever, to shout, I had no idea what.

'You know, Spérancie, I had nothing in my stomach, I was on the verge of dying of hunger, but still, I vomited. It was very bitter, just bile. I spent the night under the sink fighting with the murderers. There was a war inside my head. I think I fell asleep then was woken again almost immediately by an acute pain in my stomach. I hardly thought about my husband, all I saw were my children at the bottom of a ditch filled with bodies. I shouted loudly in French: "I will avenge you all."'

Spérancie looks at me, surprised:

'And so, Yolande? You didn't believe Emmanuelle?'

'No.'

Until my dying day, every time I think about the death of my children it will be as if I've just found out.

It seems to me at times that my life stopped that day, in the entrance hall of the Mille Collines Hotel in Kigali. I listened to Spérancie, still, petrified, without reaction. It was she who cried as she told me these horrible things. It was much later before I could cry.

I have only one hazy memory of what follows. I recall a covered lorry, around fifty of us get in. I sit on the mudguard.

They drive us under a deluge of fire to the other side of the front. At the Kimihurura roundabout the lorry stops. We stay there for a good fifteen minutes. There is a deathly silence in the lorry, detonations in the distance. It seems they're waiting for a lorry coming from the front, filled with Hutus, to do the exchange. At last, the sound of a motor. Men arguing. Discussions between Rwandan and Togolese soldiers or something like that. A man sticks his head in and stares at us briefly. Our lorry sets off once more.

We stop after another three hundred metres. Six soldiers from the RPF welcome us to the free territory. There is an explosion of joy in the lorry. People begin to sing and dance, while the lorry drives slowly towards a camp where we will be given shelter.

Sitting on my mudguard, I alone don't feel any happiness. I see my brother Nepo once more, on the evening of 6 April, when he put flour in my hand and blew it off. 'Where is the flour now?'

'Blown away,' I replied.

'Blown away. That's how your loved ones will disappear. You will lose us all and you will remain alone.'

And you, Nepo, are you dead too? You who said: 'You will soon lose everything except love. You will lose your faith, hope and confidence, but you will never lose love. And you will avenge us.'

I remain there, lost in thought, as if I'm waiting for the end of the world.

# 31

I n a few days, on 6 April 1997, the genocidaires in exile will commemorate the death of President Habyarimana who prepared the extermination of the Tutsi people in Rwanda so well.

The following day, 7 April 1997, free Rwanda will commemorate the third anniversary of the genocide.

I live in Europe, because in my country there is still no justice. Machetes wait in the shadows to slice my neck, to quiet my voice forever. No doubt, there are next to no surviving Tutsis living on my hill, Cyivugiza. Who will bear witness, if not Muganga?

But I know that one day I will return to Rwanda, my head held high.

I want to bear witness. I don't condemn anyone, I only condemn the genocide, in Rwanda and elsewhere, everywhere where people try to exterminate another people.

I've lost all of my loved ones and all of my possessions, but I couldn't care less about the possessions. Only my clinic was spared, and for good reason: it didn't belong to me. When I think of my loved ones, I'm overwhelmed with sorrow. I feel like a mother gorilla who, when her infant dies, carries it in her arms for three or four days. You know the game where you have to name as many towns as possible of a particular country? I try to name as many of my loved ones as possible who died during the genocide; a new game created for the survivors.

Christian.

Sandrine.

Nadine.

Joseph.

Hilde.

Consolata.

Nepo.

And so many more.

I hope that this testimony will give me back my lost dignity: my dignity as a woman, a mother, a nurse.

My life before the genocide is a different, distinct life. There's nothing left in my mind apart from the genocide. I've forgotten everything except the genocide. My memories were fragments that I couldn't piece back together. It was only when I was able to recount my nightmare that memories from before returned.

And now I need to talk about the genocide all of the time.

I didn't cry during the first six months – except in my sleep, I discovered. Now I can cry normally, like everyone else. But no, I'm not like everyone else yet. Right now, there is this: *life after the genocide*. People take me for someone special, delicate, who needs looking after. And I'm afraid of embarrassing them with my stories.

I want to talk about my children, my husband and the others, all the time. I want to recall my memories from before all the time. I need to talk, talk, talk, like the flow of the river Nyabarongo, where I saw so many bodies floating.

This morning it's raining in Brussels. In the tram I look at a child sitting opposite me.

My son Christian said that death must be good since you don't come back.

One day I'll be able to love completely once more. I want to have another child. I need a child like I need water.

I want to live. I want to fall in love, get pregnant, and have a beautiful child to treasure.

I want to live. It wasn't my time to die. Since death didn't want me, that is death's loss.

My dear children, two years before the massacre. From left to right, Sandrine (twelve), Christian (thirteen), Nadine (eleven). For six weeks I hoped against hope that I would find them alive.

My only remaining photograph of my husband Joseph. I found it amongst the papers at his office after the genocide. We found Joseph's body in 2006, thanks to Gacaca.

My sole photograph of my brother Nepo who predicted that I would lose all of my family but I would survive, because it was not my time to die.

Three generations: My mother has Christian on her knees, my father has the son of the mayor from their local area, I'm holding Nadine, my youngest daughter. My parents died just before the genocide. This is the same mayor who sent policemen to kill my elder sister Consolata. We still haven't found her body.

# Afterword

**D**uring the genocide, once we thought we were safe, everyone looked for food to eat. Of course. We were all dying of hunger. We'd been fleeing death for months. We'd been fleeing our old friends, sometimes even our own family members who had become killers. But I didn't search for food, I was looking for something else, probably unimportant to the others: a pen and a notebook. For me these things were crucial. I wanted to put down on paper, if possible in indelible ink, the burden I'd been carrying since the genocide began.

From the day I arrived in Belgium on 16 February 1995, I looked for a writer who could help me publish a book about my experience. My host family offered advice and assisted me with contacting a journalist who had written a book I'd just read about the genocide against the Tutsi in Rwanda.

When we met, she said: 'You lived through a terrible tragedy. But I think the best approach would be for you to tell me your story and I'll write it down.'

For once, I managed to hold back the anger I felt. 'Thank you, I'll think about it. I'll probably come back to you because I don't know anything about publishing and I'm not sure there's anyone else who can help.'

She gave me her business card and I left. But I knew in my heart of hearts that working with her would mean relinquishing control of my story, and letting the weight of my testimony be carried on the shoulders of someone who hadn't seen or lived it. It would mean betraying Joseph, Christian,

Sandrine and Nadine. Betraying you, my dear brother Nepo; you who told me that it wasn't my time to die and many other things besides. My testimony was my closest friend. I resolved that one day I would write it myself.

Given what I wanted to do, I cut the umbilical cord that tied me to my friend Lise, who nevertheless has remained a true sister of the heart, because it was thanks to her that I made it to Belgium. But I had to live my life as a survivor far away from her. My life as a refugee that I alone could understand. And I carried on writing about my life before and during the genocide. I was the only person who could make sense of my passion and pain, my solitude and despair.

I already had hundreds of pages when a Belgian friend called and asked for a favour: to collect a book from the brother of another friend based in the United States. The brother lived in Brussels like I did. My friend's last words made my heart skip: 'Apparently he writes books.' Hope! I phoned him and fixed a meeting for the next day.

'Bonjour, Monsieur. I'm Yolande Mukagasana.'

'Bonjour, Madame, I'm Patrick May. Give me a moment, I'll just go find my brother's book. Please have a seat.' A tall man, pleasant and charming.

He gave me the book and I turned to leave, explaining I had another meeting. He accompanied me to the door and at the threshold I turned and asked him: 'Is it true you write books?'

'Yes. But alas, I've never published any in the twenty-six years that I've been writing.' He sounded wounded.

'Monsieur, I have a story to publish. Have you been to Africa?'

'When I was very young, to Zaïre with my parents, but I don't know anything about Africa.'

'Have you heard about the genocide against the Tutsi in Rwanda?'

'Yes, but I can't say that I understand what happened.'

'Well, that genocide is the story I'd like us to write together. I lived through it and I've already written a manuscript.'

Patrick agreed to meet the next day at a restaurant near his flat. 'Bring your manuscript. I'll read it first, then I'll give you my response.'

Two p.m. at La Tourelle. A coffee each. I gave him fifteen pages.

'This is your manuscript?' he asked, astonished.

'No, just a part of it. These pages should be enough for you to tell whether it's worth our while working together.' I was very suspicious. He told me later that he'd noticed.

Patrick plunged into the pages straight away while I followed his reactions calmly. I understood immediately that since he didn't have many pre-existing prejudices about Africa, he'd be a good ally if he could keep his emotions under control.

After reading, he raised his eyes. I asked: 'So?'

'Madame, are you sure this is a testimony to what you lived through in Rwanda?'

'Do you think it's a horror film?'

'No, it's very powerful. I'm going to think about it and I'll let you know tomorrow. Can you bring the next pages?'

'No, Monsieur. First we'll agree on how we will work together, then we'll look at what follows. Even if we do decide to collaborate, I'll only bring you the pages we're going to work on that day because I don't want to have any surprises.'

He called me the next day and we agreed to meet that same afternoon.

'Yolande, I'm willing to work with you. But I'm afraid.'

'Why?'

'I contacted two people. I talked to the first about our meeting and he told me to be wary of Tutsi women, because they sometimes don't tell the truth. He's someone I trust. He told me to speak to a specialist on Rwanda, who no doubt you know because he's been doing research on your country for a long time, but left during the war in 1994.'

'And then?' I said, unable to hide my contempt.

'Don't be angry, I can make my own decisions. But since I don't know Africa I need more information.'

'Excuse me, Patrick. First, I want to know who gave you this information. I'm sure they lived in Rwanda before the genocide, treating my country like a cash cow, supporting those in power who killed us. It's really up to you to decide what you want to do. Either we start work or we go our separate ways.'

'What surprised me was that the last one asked me to get hold of the manuscript for him, so that he could read it and sniff out the lies. Perhaps you're right.'

We talked for a long time and in the end he told me who these two men were. I didn't have much difficulty explaining the role each one had played in my country and in my story.

He held out his hand and said to me, 'Yolande, we're going to write this book, whatever happens'.

'Perfect. What next? I don't have any money; all I have are my life and my story.'

'Neither do I. But if we publish the book, perhaps we'll make some money?'

'The money isn't the most important thing; I need the world to know what my family and my people went through. If I make money, all the better, but it's not my priority.'

We made written agreements about our collaboration, and decided that each person should send the other the agreement by registered post, and that neither of us would open their envelope until the book came out.

We worked on the manuscript for just two months and on 7 April 1997, my book, *La mort ne veut pas de moi*, saw the light of day.

My dear Patrick, may your soul be with God. You were a faithful friend, and even if some people didn't like our collaboration, you were everything I asked you to be. You helped make known the genocide perpetrated against the Tutsi in Rwanda, and the story of my family, particularly the story of my husband and my children. In spite of other pressures, you were true to your word and I applaud your bravery. I thank you from the bottom of my heart. Rest in peace.

And you dear readers, some of you will read this book with sympathy, others with regret or recrimination. What I recount is what I saw and lived. I do not hide the names of the dead. As for the names of the living, I will protect their lives and their reputations. Be they assassins or victims, I expect they will recognize themselves.

All I know is that when you destroy a life, you destroy your own too. When you kill humanity, you kill your own humanity. And then you're trapped on a path of more and more killing. When you desecrate the sacred, then you become capable of the worst.

We must learn that our differences don't have to make us enemies, they are differences to share.

Yolande Mukagasana
Rwanda, November 2018

# Translator's Note

This book was first published in French as *La mort ne veut pas de moi*, just before the third commemoration of the genocide against the Tutsi, in April 1997. Only three years had passed since Yolande Mukagasana's husband and three children had been tortured and killed a stone's throw from the family home. She was left destitute, homeless and in fear of her life. For her to transform her story into a book-length testimony so quickly was nothing short of astonishing.

In 1997 few books had appeared about the genocide, most notably *Death, Despair and Defiance* (1994) by Rakiya Omaar for African Rights, *Rwanda, histoire d'un genocide* (1994) by Colette Braeckman and *The Rwanda Crisis: History of a Genocide* (1995) by Gérard Prunier. While these texts drew on survivor testimony, this was the first book to follow the full story of one person's multifaceted experiences of genocide. It was also the first account authored by a Rwandan survivor, offering a uniquely Rwandan perspective. In her Afterword for this edition, Yolande stresses that this ownership of her own story was crucial: she worked with Patrick May on shaping the narrative, but is adamant that she maintained authorial control, portraying her version of events in her own voice. At the time this was unique. It would be another two years before fictional responses to the genocide began to appear with the publication of Ugandan novelist Goretti Kyomuhendo's *Secrets No More* (1999) and Rwandan writer John Rusimbi's *By the Time She Returned* (1999); and three years before another survivor testimony was published, Marie-Aimable Umurerwa's *La langue entre les dents* (The Tongue Between the Teeth, 2000).

*Not My Time to Die* is extraordinary not only because it was the first Rwandan-authored book-length testimony but also because its narrative is emotionally complex and stylistically daring. Yolande Mukagasana often thinks and recounts her story in dialogue. She peoples her account with the voices of others: her family and friends who died, those who helped her and those who wanted to kill her. This is unusual for testimony, which usually relies more on the survivor's memories of their own perceptions at the time and less on reconstructed conversations. I was staying at Yolande's house in Nyamata when she wrote the Afterword for this edition, overnight, in one sitting. She recalled a vivid mixture of details (times, locations), feelings (suspicion, anger, disappointment) and word-for-word conversations in a style that echoed her earlier testimony. Talking to me about her first drafts of the book, she explained: 'I wrote it as if I was talking to the paper'. The reader today may feel like a listener, following events as they unfold, almost in real time.

I first read *La mort ne veut pas de moi* in 2006 when I was studying for a PhD in African literature at SOAS. Six years later, during a two-month stay in Rwanda, someone told me Yolande had returned to Kigali from Brussels and gave me her phone number. We met in a private room of a bar in Nyamirambo one Sunday: Yolande, her second husband Régis and a family friend. Three hours later we had a collection of empty bottles and the sense that this might be the start of a friendship. A few years after that first meeting, I asked Yolande if she would be willing to let me translate the text and in June 2015, when my first son was five months old, I completed the first chapter. It would take me three years (and another baby) before the first draft was finished. As I learned to be a mother myself I gradually came to understand some of the enormity of her loss. In the process I discovered the ways my own mind had tricked me in my reading. I consistently forgot the contents of

Chapter Thirty, the chapter that recounts the way Christian, Sandrine and Nadine are killed, and it wasn't until I translated it word by word, in January 2018, that I was finally able to hear the end of their story.

Translation across languages, cultures and two decades raises multiple questions. Yolande and I answered these in dialogue; at times in person, sitting around a table on her terrace at home, her cat Kunda winding between our ankles, at other times by phone. We were lucky to find so much time to discuss the text's transformation, working as we were for most of the journey without a book contract and with little understanding of the translation rights! Rwandan publisher Huza Press came on board enthusiastically in the summer of 2018, aligning with our desire to reach English-speaking Rwandan audiences first and foremost and in tune with the book's ethos of East African authorship and independence. Doreen Baingana, Ugandan literary activist and prize-winning author of *Tropical Fish*, agreed to edit the testimony and transformed the text once more: challenging us to question the purpose of each word, the relevance of the material today and the different idiosyncrasies of English and French.

So what did we change? Firstly, Doreen and I sought clarifications. There was some missing information, such as the name of the village where Yolande was born, Sandrine's age, the nature of the first killings. Sometimes the style created ambiguities in the original. For example, towards the end of Chapter One when Yolande thinks about different songs that depict Rwanda's land and people, the evocative internal monologue moved seamlessly between work by different musicians in the original French, but we separated it out for clarity in the translation. There were also puzzles I wished to explore further. 'Why did all the milk in Rwanda turn sour?' I asked, referring to the childhood memories of violence in Chapter Three. Yolande explained that after she was wounded by men looking for her father, they went on to attack the family's milking cow. After seeing the slaughtered animal, every time she drank milk she tasted blood. Cows, a sign of wealth originally linked to the Tutsi ethnicity, are highly symbolic in Rwanda. So we decided to include this new material in the English translation.

Other mysteries we didn't explain. I've always been puzzled by the first paragraph of the book where Yolande discusses the rebellious nature of the Rwandan soul. So much of the academic literature about genocide focuses on Rwandan deference to authority, on the way in which ordinary people complied with orders to kill coming from above. Why then open a book about genocide with this assertion of independence? 'Comprenne qui pourra' she writes in the original, understand this if you can. Today I see the rebellion as twofold. On the one hand are the Tutsis who refused to die, who resisted being wiped out of existence. On the other are the ordinary people who were told to kill but instead (or in addition) helped in various small ways, resisting orders by protecting their neighbours, sometimes in spite of themselves. Even when there is apparent uniformity (neighbours killed neighbours) people still make individual choices. Or so I think. Perhaps you read it differently?

As languages, French and English each have their own personalities and publishing cultures. English-language books for general audiences are usually heavily edited to remove redundancies, repetitions and ambiguity. Experienced translators, such as Sarah Ardizzone, have suggested that French editors may work with a lighter touch, and books such as this one that were published in haste may have hardly been changed from submission to publication. As such, Doreen Baingana recommended edits to remove repetitions, particularly those that 'told' the reader about a situation that was then recounted in a way that 'showed' what was meant. At other points, however, we kept repetitions because they formed a deliberate stylistic choice for communicating intense emotion. We made similar decisions about the use of very short sentences and different tenses, smoothing out variations that didn't contribute to the purpose of the storytelling but keeping unusual grammar when it did serve the narrative ends, for example the use of the present tense when Emmanuelle and Spérancie recount terrible sights of violence.

We also made efforts in the English translation to present information about events as Yolande would have heard or interpreted them from her hiding position, rather than through the voice of an omniscient narrator, which sometimes creeps into the French original. In Chapter Fourteen, for example, Yolande hides under Mzee's bed at Pauline and Déo's house. Stressed by the RPF bombardment, Déo, in a fit of fear and rage, storms off to look for her under Emmanuelle's sink, where she had been hiding until very recently. The French original describes him walking across the compound as if he is being seen. We rephrased this so that the account of what happens is conveyed through what is heard. This didn't change the content of the narrative but did reinforce the realism of the text, moving from an extrapolation created by Patrick and Yolande from her memories and conversations with others back to an in-the-moment account of what she was able to perceive at the time.

Some words and phrases don't move between languages easily: they need to be changed to preserve their original meaning. So, for example, the French word 'refugié' might appear to have an easy English correlation in 'refugee' but in practice the French is more flexible. 'Refugié' can signify a person who has left their country or region, fleeing danger. The English 'refugee' (derived from French), on the other hand, signifies someone who has crossed a *national border* to escape war, persecution or natural disaster. The women and children hiding in the Nyamirambo parish buildings and in the Centre of Saint Paul were not therefore strictly speaking refugees. In English we might refer to them as internally displaced persons but this language seems overly legal for a testimonial narrative. So instead, I translated every iteration of 'refugié' in the original with descriptions of the people most relevant for the context. This turned out to be a humanizing gesture, particularly given the current media homogenization of refugees.

The title of the book also proved difficult to translate. *La mort ne veut pas de moi* literally means 'Death Doesn't Want Me'. This is not an idiomatic phrase in English so we looked for another title that would maintain this sense of fate and the connection to Nepo's prophecy. After much discussion we settled on *Not My Time to Die*. This is not an ideal solution: something of the forlorn rejection and personification of death inherent in 'Death Doesn't Want Me' is lost. But the French title was already a compromise: the book was originally called *Les larmes d'une mère*, 'A Mother's Tears'. No title can capture the rich complexity of the testimony that follows.

One of the major motivations for this translation was that Rwanda has moved from promoting French as the international language of business and education to favouring English. This was in part due to revulsion at France's role in the genocide and in part in order to align Rwanda with other East African Anglophone countries. Because young people no longer grow up learning French at school, a whole generation of young Rwandans had not been able to read this important book. Our most important audience for the translation, then, is Rwandans themselves. This informed many of our choices. For example, in the French edition most proverbs are given only in translation, but in this new edition, Yolande and I decided to return to the original Kinyarwanda alongside English translations. Equally, some widely understood Kinyarwanda terms are used throughout, such as 'Interahamwe' for the local militia. We decided to use the Kinyarwanda word 'Mama' rather than the English 'Mummy' or 'Mother' as a translation for 'Maman'.

In the existing literature available in English from and about Rwanda, such Kinyarwanda words and phrases are nearly always presented in italics, a convention that has historically been used by international publishers to signal the presence of a 'foreign' language that is presumed to be unfamiliar for the reader. This convention clearly didn't make sense for this edition of Yolande Mukagasana's testimony: a testimony written by a Rwandan survivor for Rwandan readers. Italics tend to render the language they signal strange, implying a change of voice or tone. However, in Rwanda, Kinyarwanda is the first language for the vast majority of the population and for many switching between languages – Kinyarwanda, English, Kiswahili, French – is common, even within the same sentence. In keeping with an emerging trend in wider African literary publishing, we therefore chose not to italicize Kinyarwanda words or phrases in this book. This includes proverbs because rather than being unchanging citations, here they are incorporated playfully in daily language. See for example the references to hyenas in this book that at times reference a specific proverb in full, at other times rework it creatively.

The renewed focus on the Rwandan context for this edition helped to solve many of my translation difficulties. I would spend days trying to work with an elaborate metaphor only to find, when asking Yolande for help, that she would say 'Oh, that was Patrick!' and we'd agree to change it or take it out. So, for example, I removed the simile of the snow-capped volcano looking like a dancer's tutu because Rwandan classical dance features no such costume. At other times there were stories behind the descriptions that justified leaving them as they were. For example, the cries of kites are described as 'petits hennissements' or little neighs at the opening of Chapter Twenty-Five. At the point of writing the book Yolande explained she'd only ever seen one horse in her life! The word found its way into the text because Patrick asked Yolande to mimic these particular bird calls so he could describe them for the reader: the analogy was his. This remembered scene of Yolande mimicking the birds' cries and Patrick scribbling down words was too evocative to lose. So I've kept the description as 'whinnying cries'.

Finally, as I translated, I updated some elements of the text for Rwandan and international audiences. Twenty-five years after the events the book recounts, Rwanda has come a long way. What was referred to as the Rwandan genocide when this book was published is now called the 1994 genocide against the Tutsi in Rwanda. The new wording, agreed nationally by the Rwandan government and internationally by the UN, aims to clarify who was killed, working against genocide denial and revisionism. As such, even though it would have been truer to the original to use the phrase 'Rwandan genocide', I updated it to the new wording throughout, because this is so crucial for memory work in the present.

Other words have changed in the language for various reasons. In 1994, while the UK press referred to people from Rwanda as 'Rwandan', most English-speakers in the countries surrounding Rwanda called them 'Rwandese'. Indeed the Rwandan Patriotic Front was originally named the Rwandese Patriotic Front and was referred to as such by Prunier, among others. While translating I could have used 'Rwandese' throughout. However, I worried that this would make the book feel like it was coming from a distant time in the past, when in fact many of the observations are still relevant today. So I have used 'Rwandan' throughout. Other small words have also been changed. Yolande originally referred to the child 'Joker', who she encounters tied up and starving when she flees Emmanuelle's house in Chapter Sixteen, as 'débile' or 'mentally defective'. Disability rights campaigners argue that the use of such words is profoundly wounding. So, in discussion with Yolande, I changed the adjective to a longer description of the challenges he faced: 'a child who has always had trouble learning'.

The most significant change we made in updating the text was to cut several paragraphs comparing 'black savagery' and 'white barbarity' from the opening of Chapter Twelve. While editing, Doreen Baingana suggested these paragraphs might actually reinforce racist ideas rather than refute them. I observed that they were written at a time when the genocide against the Tutsi was still sometimes being dismissed as 'the usual tribal infighting'. However, more than two decades later the discourse about Rwanda has changed and the genocide is regularly discussed in relation to the Holocaust and later genocides in Cambodia, Bosnia and Darfur. What still horrifies is that the UN didn't take action to stop the killing. This point seemed to be intricately intertwined with Yolande's comments about white and black violence. So, after discussion with

Yolande, I changed the order of the chapter to begin with her description of the UN driving through Nyamirambo, then moving on to discuss relationships between Rwandans and white Europeans.

The paratext also required some reflection. The original French edition begins with an 'Avertissement au lecteur' or 'Note to the Reader' purportedly from Yolande Mukagasana. Intriguingly, Yolande didn't identify with the note's account of her as a woman who lives in the spoken rather than the written word, nor did the idea that her only friend was her testimony still resonate. So she suggested cutting it out. She wrote the Afterword as a replacement, but one that we placed at the end rather than the beginning of the text so that her testimony takes centre stage. We similarly cut the very out-of-date chronology that was found at the end of the text, aware that contemporary histories of Rwanda are now widely available.

While the events described in this book take place in 1994, it remains as fresh, urgent and relevant today as it was when it first appeared in 1997. In the face of genocide denial, survivor testimonies become ever more important, both as evidence and to help communicate the human cost of violence. When I interviewed Gaël Faye about his novel *Petit Pays (Small Country)* he told me this was the first book he read about the genocide against the Tutsi, a genocide he'd lived through at distance in exile in Burundi with his Rwandan mother and family. As he explains on the cover, Yolande's book made the genocide feel real and personal. I first encountered Yolande through her testimony, then as an academic through our conversations about her work and finally as a translator weighing each of her words, debating the meaning of a particular phrase together, trying to capture the spirit of the French original as I'd come to understand it over the years. The unbearable pain of loss in these pages never dulls. Nor does her courage and compassion.

Zoe Norridge

**Yolande Mukagasana** is a renowned Rwandan writer, public figure and campaigner for the remembrance of the 1994 genocide against the Tutsi. She has authored four books about genocide and its aftermath, performed her testimony in the iconic Rwanda 94 touring theatre production and has received numerous international prizes for her work, including the Alexander Langer Foundation Prize for Testimony and Solidarity, the American Jewish Committee Moral Courage Award and an Honourable Mention for the UNESCO Education for Peace Prize. Her first book, *La mort ne veut pas de moi*, has been translated into Italian, Turkish, Norwegian, Danish, Dutch, Hebrew and now English.

**Zoe Norridge** is a Senior Lecturer in African and Comparative Literature at King's College London. She researches cultural responses to the genocide against the Tutsi in Rwanda, collaborates with Rwandan artists and genocide educators, appears on radio discussing the arts in Rwanda and is Chair of the Ishami Foundation.

**Huza Press editorial team**
Louise Umutoni Bower and Kate Wallis, Co-Directors
Doreen Baingana, Editor
Otieno Owino, Copy Editor
Lucky Grace Isingizwe, Communications
Robert Harries and Emma-Claudine Ntirenganya, Proofs

Printed in the United States
By Bookmasters